THINK-LEAP

Is the grass on the other side greener? Or is it really dead?

-REGRET

L. Rogers

outskirtspress

DENVER, COLORADO

Outskirts Press, Inc.
http://www.outskirtspress.com

ISBN: 978-1-4787-0767-7

Outskirts Press and the "OP" logo are trademarks belonging to Outskirts Press, Inc.

PRINTED IN THE UNITED STATES OF AMERICA

Table of Contents

CHAPTER 1

The Beginning Of The End

"WHERE HAVE YOU been?" I yelled at my wife as she walked through the front door. The cool air together with the drizzle chilled my whole body as the door opened and closed. This was on a cold and rainy Sunday morning in the middle of February. My wife had been gone since six o' clock a.m. to work in the small retail store she owned. We spoke around three o' clock p.m. to discuss the plans we made the night before. She said she was at the grocery store when we last spoke. She was supposed to be home within that next hour. It was then one o' clock a.m. the next morning. I hugged her though she was reluctant to hug back.

"We've been worried sick about you, I haven't heard from you in hours. Are you all right?"

She didn't say a word. Her face was loaded with despair as she pulled away and walked into the kitchen. I followed and watched her get a glass of water. She leaned backwards against the countertop as she drank.

"We've been worried about you," I said once more, "I've been calling everywhere to see if anybody heard from you."

"I told you not to do that to me!" she yelled. "It's none of their business what's going on with me. What's wrong with you?"

She nudged me as she stormed by and went into our bedroom. Wearied and confused, I went into the living room and sat on the sofa attempting to make sense of what was happening.

That had never happened before. In times past, we did our best to keep in touch when we were away for long periods of time. We always knew each other's location and what the other spouse was doing. There were no problems when we got home. But on that particular Saturday, she went to work and we last spoke around three o' clock. We had plans to have a family night in with the children. There were supposed to be games, movies, and home cooking which was to start at five o' clock. There actually were games, movies, and a home cooked meal. Minus her of course. We waited on her until seven. The children started asking questions of her whereabouts, so I decided to begin the night. This would help occupy their minds; as it did. They all fell asleep around ten thirty and I got no rest at all.

Thirty minutes had passed and I was still sitting on the sofa contemplating. Contemplating how to approach her and find out what happened without starting a war. She looked very upset and uneasy when she went into the bedroom. She slammed the door behind her. Experience had taught me to never come at her in a straight forward manner when she's in that mode. I might have ended up in a day long argument that would have been impossible for me to win.

Nevertheless, a few minutes later I decided to step into the fire. I hesitated when I got to the bedroom door because she was talking to someone on the phone. Sounded like a family member on the other end. The conversation seemed to be serious because she was crying. The first thing that came to mind was she had a fight with a relative or a friend. I've seen it before. When it happens, her emotions become like a wrecked ship. It's worse than with an argument with me. For days I would have to endure heavy tears, snappy responses, and sometimes complete silence. In some cases, it took weeks for her to get over it. I thought we were headed for another one of those moments on that cold and rainy night in February. Man was I wrong!

So I opened the door and heard her say, "I'm gonna go ahead and tell him ok. I'll talk to you later. Goodbye."

Her eyes were almost completely dry of tears by the time

she put down the phone. I should have been relieved but something was wrong. There was an awful feeling in the air like never before. I watched her as she turned from me and stared at a picture on the nightstand. A photo we took together and had two smaller copies made into key chains. We appeared to be a couple of happy souls packed into our own little happy box. She even took a poem, I wrote for her, and placed it in the frame to use as a backdrop for the photo. People saw it and thought we were the perfect couple.

She continued to stare silently at the picture. Her focusing on it seemed to have blotted out everything else around her. I think she forgot I was there too until I spoke.

"Baby what's wrong?" I asked softly.

Without saying a word, she lowered her head slightly.

"Everything all-right?" I asked.

She sighed, raised her head slowly, and looked toward but not directly at me. Her eyes never made contact with mine when she said, "we need to talk. I think we should go into the living room."

Everybody in this world has a fear of something. We are afraid of some things more than we are of others. But there is a moment in life when something frightens us most of all. I believe that was my most frightful moment. The sound of her voice and the feeling in the air scared me to death. The trip from the bedroom to the living room sofa felt like that final walk to the execution chamber and my wife was ready to throw the switch. I came in and sat down beside her. She grabbed my hands and began to speak.

"Baby," she said as she looked directly into my eyes, "I did something today and it's killing me inside. I never did anything like this before and I can't get it off my mind. I thought about not telling you but it's something I gotta do to clear my conscience."

At that moment, I was terrified. What could she have done that was so horrible? Should we be expecting company because of some crime she's committed? All I could ask her was, "did somebody get hurt or something?"

She said, "Yes."

"She can't be serious!" I thought to myself. "Who?" I asked.

"Myself, and I'm sure it's gonna hurt you too."

That made me wonder which mode I should be in. I didn't know, so I listened as she continued to speak.

"Remember when I called you earlier?" she asked.

"Yeah, I remember. You called around three."

"Well," she sighed and lowered her head slightly, "I said I was at the grocery store. Baby, that wasn't true. I've been at my store up until the time I left and came here."

"Why?" I asked with infused curiosity. Ten years of marriage and that was the first time I could recall her lying to me. But the real hurt was yet to come.

"I was outside putting some things in the car an hour before we spoke," she said. "I was on the way back in when someone stopped me. This person needed to speak with me before I left the store tonight. I began closing up and was about to come home. Before I could lock the door, he walked in," she paused and lowered her head some more.

"Who walked in?" I asked.

She remained silent.

"Who was it?" I asked with a bit more aggression.

"You remember that guy I told you about? The guy that came in looking for a gift for his mom and girlfriend back in November."

"Yeah I know em!" I said. "That's you and your mom's new found friend, right! So you're telling me you stayed there ten extra hours talking to him about gifts!"

"Not exactly."

"Why then?" I yelled slightly. Really, I didn't wanna hear the answer to that question. Deep down inside, I could feel sorrow approaching. She was looking directly into my face at that time as she continued to speak.

"Please don't be mad at me when I tell you this," she said with a shaky voice. "You know we've been having problems the last few months and tonight, I wasn't thinking clearly."

We've had issues like every other couple. It comes with the territory. Some people are capable of solving any problem that comes their way while others can't solve the simplest. I think we've done a pretty good job over the years. We've often heard people tell us, "You two don't seem to have any problems. Looks like you have the perfect marriage." If only they knew we kept everything in-house. We learned years ago to keep our business to ourselves. Yes, we've had issues; then what made that night different from all the others?

"I talked with him right before I called you," she continued, "He did something that caught me by surprise. He said he has developed feelings for me over the last three months. He realizes it's wrong cause I'm married, but he can't help himself."

"Wait a minute!" I interrupted. "Guys hit on you like this all the time. They pretty much say the same thing. It never bothered you before."

"I know, but that wasn't all he said. He went much further. It's like he knew exactly what I wanted to hear."

"Baby I'm puzzled," I said, "What are you really saying to me? Are you telling me this man's words caused you to lie to me and stay out all night?"

"Not only his words, but the things he did too. Sweety I'm so sorry. I let him get to me and almost allowed my emotions to get caught up. Please don't be angry with me when I tell you this."

As you can imagine, my mind was all over the place. I wanted to just stop her from talking; knowing pain was on the way. She felt a need to tell me so I kept listening.

"He told me how beautiful I was and any man would want me. He talked about things he would do to me to make me feel good and forget about all my problems. I know this is gonna hurt you more than it already has. And again I'm sorry. I lied to you because I enjoyed it. I wanted to stay there all night and listen to all he had to say to me. He made me feel something I never felt before."

I wanted to explode but endured instead. She said he left

the store to give her privacy while she called me. He came right back after we were done talking. He continued to speak the words she wanted to hear. He even touched her. He brushed her hair with the back of his hand. He caressed her arm as well as her thigh.

Already in shock and turmoil, what she said next completely broke my heart. When your heart gets broken, believe it or not, you actually feel it. It's like a sharp pain that tears right through the middle of it. It was the worst pain I'd ever felt.

"While he was talking," she said, "all I could do was close my eyes and take it all in. He spoke into my ear and all I could see was me and him in bed making passionate love. I wanted him to touch me in any way he pleased. He made me completely forget I was married. Then I came to my senses."

Each word spoken after her saying, "all I could see was", felt like the stroke from a jackhammer pounding my heart. The pain got worse after each word. I was hearing something I thought would never be spoken by any wife of mine. Something not even remotely close to it.

She went on to say, "I know I told you he wanted to hang out in the store with us and only wanted to be friends. I wanted to be friends with him too. But I started having a crush on him, even though he's not near my type. He just reminds me so much of Dad. The way he dresses and talks, and the way he carries himself. He's so clean and neat just like my dad was. He told me when I get home, to make love to you and think about him."

She began to speak as if she had justification for doing this. That infuriated me.

"How could you do this to me?" I yelled. "All these years I never did anything like this to you! What were you thinking?"

"You caused this!" she yelled back. "OH, you forgot about what you did to me the other day? You said you wouldn't do it again remember!"

"I told you I didn't do it, why won't you believe me? You know I'm telling the truth!"

Some months back, I did something awful that hurt her both

physically and emotionally. She became ill for a while. Before it was all over though, I had the most regret. Much more than she had, and it still bothers me until this day. She realized what took place happens to a lot of people. Although she felt it wasn't that big of an issue when it was over, I promised to never do it again; which I didn't. She didn't believe me and it must have been a big deal again. She argued with me about it that whole week and failed to notice the sickness never returned; which proved that I was telling the truth.

"I told you what would happen if you keep doing the things you do," she said.

"I told you I didn't do that again!" I yelled.

"I'm not just talking about that, think about the other things. You don't compliment me; you never tell me what I wanna hear. I know what I did tonight was wrong, but I was tired. I told you if you don't do these things, some other man will."

First of all, I've always complimented her. From the time we met and then on. She just didn't hear me when I did it for some reason! She sure had no problem hearing compliments from other men. She would always come home in a really good mood when some guy called her pretty. Man, she rubbed it in my face each time!

"How could you talk like this after what you did tonight?" I yelled.

"Well, I didn't have to open up and tell you, did I? I could have kept it a secret and let it happen again if I wanted it to," she said in a lower tone of voice.

She was right. That's something I needed to think about. Apparently she still cared about our marriage. She didn't have to tell me what happened and could have allowed it to continue on without me knowing. Telling me was for the best though. If I'd found out later, on my own, no telling what may have happened. Angry would have been an understatement. There's people doing life in prison or dead because their spouse or mate wasn't honest with them. The cheating got discovered. Some of them I know or knew personally.

The more she talked the more she sounded remorseful. Her right state of mind was returning. That eased my heartache just a little bit. However, the pain would be completely gone as soon as I got my hands on this fellow. What man wouldn't enjoy pounding on the guy that touched his wife? Fortunately for him, that wasn't ever gonna happen. She said that she was sorry and he would be told not to bother her again. Telling him wasn't good enough for me.

"You know what," I said, "let me rough em up a little. I guarantee he'll leave you alone!"

"No!" she said. "Don't go up there starting trouble. I'll handle this my way. He won't bother me no more."

"Yeah, but he'll see how serious you are about it when I get my hands on him. He'll know it's open season on him and he won't come back."

"No! I know how to handle this," she claimed. "I don't need you at my store causing a big scene. It will hurt the business. Promise me you won't do this. Please promise me!"

We discussed and argued about this for about ten more minutes. I finally gave in after she burst into tears. Could never resist her demands when she cried like that. I promised as I held and comforted her. Once again she apologized and said she would never do this again. That may have been the most sincere I've ever seen her. The passion in her voice helped me accept that she made a human mistake.

"We all make mistakes," I said, "we'll get through this like all the other problems that came our way."

"I know we will," she said.

It was well past two, still we continued to talk. She eventually dosed off, used my lap as a pillow, and stretched across the sofa. She slept like a baby. All seemed well but wasn't. My heart was still broken and I was restless. In fact, I don't think I got an hour of sleep that night. That was the first time I had ever lost sleep over anything. My mind was still boggled and my thoughts were bouncing all over the place. Where did I go wrong? Was this all real? What can I do to make sure this won't happen again? Is this really a nightmare? My wife did not do this to me! Maybe someone else's wife, but not mine! This can't happen to me! My wife and my marriage are too good for this!

I was hoping denial would help me relax. It worked for a while then reality returned. I could not get it off my mind. I thought I was losing it and went into the bedroom and lied down for a spell. I remember sleeping for only a brief moment. The pain started all over again when I awoke. I kept telling my-self everything is gonna be okay but, couldn't help sensing more trouble on the way.

That Sunday morning was a cold and sunny one. The sun pierced through the curtains and I thought about that terrible night I had survived. The new question was; what was next? No rest and no sleep, still, fatigue hadn't set in yet. It was around seven in the morning. My children were up into their morning routines. They had no idea what happened the night before. We were one big happy family as far as they were concerned. They didn't get to see us argue the night before. Sometimes, they knew when there was a problem between us. They could tell when one or both of us were mad with the other. Guess it wasn't showing at the time.

My wife seemed enthused as she arose and prepared for church. As for me, going to church was the last thing on my mind. In fact, I was feeling betrayed by the church and what we were taught there over the years. (Never let anybody or any-thing come between your marriage.) I felt that's exactly what she did, although we were still together. It's just the thought of her having feelings for another man.

"You going to church today?" she asked.

"Don't feel like it," I answered.

"Come on, please! I know I put you through a tough time last night and I know I hurt you. Going to church will only make you feel better, it'll only help us. Come on!"

"I don't think so," I said.

She had to be feeling really good that morning. She sat on my lap and gave me a long sensuous kiss. That alone made me forget about my troubles. Yes! We went to church and things were back on track. What a weekend!

She began the week by having that discussion with this guy. He didn't take it well when he was told not to bother her anymore. She said he insisted on being her friend even after being told it wasn't a good idea. I've never heard of a friendship between a man and a woman, in which at least one was attracted to the other, that didn't eventually become a romantic one. We see it all the time. If you continue being friends, it's gonna happen sooner or later. Even if one or both of them say it will never happen. You hang-out long enough, you will become lovers. It's human nature.

He told her he'll still come into the store to purchase things whether she was his friend or not. If it was up to me, he wouldn't have come within five miles of the store. But I promised not to get involved. Besides, she handled her business quite well. I was proud of her. He wasn't seen for the rest of the week.

Business was as usual at the store. I sat in for her on days when she had other matters to attend to. I knew how things were to proceed since I helped set it up. The problem was, I hadn't spent a lot of time there and didn't exactly know what to expect from customers and the other shop owners. Man did I find out fast!

They consisted of a variety of personalities. Most were regulars who frequent the store daily, which also included some of the other business owners. I had no problems with first time customers; wish I could say the same about those regulars. They let me know that they did not appreciate me being there. It took me a while to find out why, but I did. Imagine how it feels to greet someone with a "hello", or a "how are you doing", and not get a response back. You go out of the way to be nice to them and get treated like scum. Some never spoke to me the whole time I was there. I picked my face up off the counter daily.

Then there are those who did speak, but very harshly toward me. Yeah, we had friendly conversations; but are we not supposed to be in a pleasant mood afterwards? They made me feel like a child being scolded and yelled at. These folks were completely rude and nasty!

There were also the ones that tried to pick information from me. They knew I was the owner's husband and tried to get more info about her. They wanted to know about our life at home. The blockheads even tried to get me to talk about the guy who tried to interfere with my marriage. Most of them knew him personally. I figured they only wanted to cause more trouble. I blew them off the first chance I got.

My wife explained why all those people treated me so cold-heartedly. They all wanted to date her. I never saw anything like it before. It made them jealous when they saw the owner's spouse running the store. Who could blame them? She's a very beautiful and intelligent young woman. Even some of the women there made passes at her. I'm guessing they were lesbians, right! The whole ordeal was hilarious until she said they did the same thing to him. That bothered me. This guy hung around so much; it caused them to believe she was already dating him. He almost got into a physical confrontation with one of them. He walked in and saw this other guy leaning on the counter talking with her. Guess he got jealous. They exchanged words and threats over another man's wife. Imagine that! It made me wanna pack up everything and move her to a new location. That wasn't my call though.

Business got better as each day without drama went by. The store gained popularity throughout the whole city and became a magnet for out of town patrons. Whenever there was some big event in town, profits for that day increased by one hundred percent or more. Sometimes we stayed open hours past closing in order to satisfy every customer. People soon began hiring her to setup and coordinate special occasions such as weddings and birthday parties. I found myself working another fulltime job, with no wages. Either I was working in the store, or moving and setting up equipment. I did what any loving husband would have done to support his wife's business endeavors.

Working together made our life at home great. The rat that tried to come between us hadn't been spoken of for weeks. Not since she told him to leave her alone. It was healthy for us. The absence of bitter quarrels and grown-ups yelling at each other was even better for the kids. Children seem to be happier and perform better at school when there are no negative distractions at home. More of our time was being spent with them. Yes, the perfect household! If someone had told me it wasn't going to last, I wouldn't have believed them.

The busier she got, the less we saw of each other. My work-load lessened as hers increased. It was her ship and she was the captain. I worked when, where, and how she told me to. She hired more help, which was understandable. It was needed. My schedule went from daily to Wednesdays only. That gave me more time to spend with my children. More time for parks and video games. More of me and less of their mom! She became so involved in her work, that even I would only see her one or maybe two hours a day. It got frustrating fast. Especially when she came home late one night and dropped some items off. She took a shower and disappeared again. I wasn't all that con-cerned because she had friends with her. On top of that, she became adamant with keeping in touch with us since that cold Saturday night. We knew where she was at all times. Still, not seeing her as much got frustrating.

One Friday, we wanted to surprise her. My children and I came up to the store unannounced. Boy was she surprised. You should have seen the look on her face when she turned around after hearing small voices calling her mommy. It was like she heard and saw a ghost.

"What are you doing here?" she asked as they wrapped their arms around her.

"You surprised?" I asked.

"Yeah! But you could have called."

She seemed a bit jumpy. She kept looking around the whole time. It was around five o'clock that afternoon and the store was unusually empty for that particular day of the week. Come to think of it, Fridays were the busiest.

"Where is everybody?" I asked.

"Uh, it's been pretty slow today," she said nervously.

"Slow on a Friday, that's strange. Maybe they gambled up all their money at the casinos!" I joked.

She laughed slightly. "Hey," she said, "you think you can watch the store for a while? I need to step out and handle something. Please!"

"Of course I could," I said delightfully," go and handle your business."

She left while we made ourselves at home. Not one customer came into the store. Only got nasty looks from a couple of regulars who walked by. I agreed to this because I figured it would only take a few minutes, considering the time. I was approximately four hours wrong. She didn't get back until after nine.

"I'm sorry everybody!" she said as the children ran to hug her. "I didn't know it was gonna take so long." She appeared calm, unlike earlier. Thinking about attending to that business must have made her nervous.

"It's ok," I said, "You did what you had to do. Besides, the kids haven't been here for a while. They needed to get back familiar with the shop." So we closed up and left.

They rode in her car as we drove home. With the exception of her working so much, there were no worries in our household. She was as loving as a wife and mother could be right then.

That being said, the next few months will be the most difficult period of my life. People who have experienced this will understand completely. I'll get around to discussing that difficult period, but first, two chapters of history.

CHAPTER 2

A Snake, A Weasel, Or A Wolf

SOME CALL HIM a snake. Others call him a weasel. He's also been known as a wolf in sheep's clothing. Whichever you decide to call him, all remains the same. He's still cunning, deceitful, and treacherous. Takes advantage of any individual not aware of his intentions. We've all encountered this person before. He's the drug addict on the corner pretending to be in need of food. Or the mechanic who tells you there's more wrong with your car than there really is. He's the one sending emails concerning his fortune. He needs to deposit it into your bank account, hoping to get your personal info to exploit your identity. Yeah, we've all had to deal with him. That same ole snake, weasel, and wolf. Unfortunately, he brought mess our way, my wife and me. You know him! The guy I discussed earlier who tried to invade our marriage. Let me tell you how she first met him.

I wasn't there, but I was told he came into my wife's store one morning looking for gifts. This took place at the beginning of November, just a few months after the grand opening. He was from out of town and needed something to impress his girlfriend and a gift for his mother. My wife had the perfect gifts for him. What made her shop so unique was the selection of hot items, difficult to find elsewhere, and those unusual ones that only she had. The store also carried a ton of antique and vintage home decors. She's also a gift basket expert. Of course they were odd too. There were two on display that caught his eye. Rather than buying those, he wanted her to make two more similar to them. They were to be picked up the following week. He even paid extra for them; that's what sparked the friendship.

The thing that really got them conversing was her interest in a hat he was wearing. She wanted to know where he got it so she could try to stock them in her store. He said he could arrange a meeting with her and the supplier. They exchanged numbers and she could call when ready to set up the deal. After the meeting, they began having friendly phone sessions. He continued to visit the store, three times a week on the days his job brought him to town.

"Coming in here makes my day every time. You give me all the energy I need," he said to my wife.

He was a distinguished fellow and apparently quite charming. He looked to be in his mid thirties and in good shape. Clean cut and well dressed, sporting his own style of attire. He was outspoken and always had interesting conversations. He was a businessman owning property in multiple states. An eligible bachelor who had never been married! This guy was cool; everybody wanted to be a part of his entourage. I hadn't met him yet and was only hearing about him during that time. He was good at what he was doing or trying to do. I was almost fooled by him too, but, thank GOD for making me a good judge of character.

Analyzing his personality, after it was described to me, helped me to develop my own opinion about him. Everything spoken about him was all the ingredients of a snake, a weasel, or a wolf. Was I right? We'll find out later on.

Women were attracted to this guy mainly because, "he has himself together," they all claimed. His career, finances, personality, etc. More of them started visiting the store on the days he was in town, desperate for his attention. It turned into a competition and he was the big prize. Sometimes they would come into the store and hang around until he showed up. They'd come in and talk to my wife as if they were looking for her companionship. She knew it was all an act just to get to him. The moment he showed up, their attitudes toward her did a

360 degree turn. She was deemed a threat because they saw him talking to her all the time. They felt all interest was focused on her. My wife later discovered that he even spoke about her among these women. Nothing bad was said, all good things. How do you think that made them feel? She was just an innocent victim dragged into a senseless contest. She had no interest in being with him romantically at all. It was all about business and conversation.

Two things I despise in this world are arrogance and constant boasting. It's one thing to have confidence in yourself, but this guy was a world of self-importance.

"He just ignited one day!" my wife told me. "Just started bragging on himself and his possessions."

She said he talked about where he was from and how people there adored him. They gave him the red carpet treatment like he was royalty or a mega star. Everything he has is the best, better than everyone else's. The two houses he owns in his hometown are spectacular. They're built with the best materials and contain the most expensive furniture and decorations. When people visit, they never wanna leave. They ask if they could have their next party or get-together at one of the houses.

His three vehicles were personally suited up by him. Everyone that owns a car in his neighborhood envies him. All eyes are on him as he drives down the street. Some automobile collectors offered big bucks for them but he wasn't selling. He owned a ranch in Texas that housed the best bred horses. The world's best wardrobe was his. He won any and every dance contest he'd ever entered. Women flirted with him because he has such a perfect body. He had to wear oversized clothing when his friends came over. That was done to keep their girlfriends and wives from noticing his well chiseled abdomen and perfectly shaped legs. He didn't want them to leave their men because of him.

What a guy! Right! I didn't believe any of it. I thought it was all a bunch of garbage. He reminded me of one of my co-workers who did the same thing just for attention. My wife started believing this guy so I had to intervene with this story.

This co-worker of mine started boasting the day he began working with us. From the gourmet meals he ate everyday to the mansion he owned in a prominent part of town. His property was so large that he installed a mini park on it. It included a full basketball court which dominated his daily conversation. He owned two luxury cars, a black and a white one, which were exactly the same make, model, and year. One day he'd drive the black one to work, the next day the white. The life of a made-man was his. He really wanted us to believe that. Actually, what he told us really was the truth. All these things he did own, well, not exactly. All of it could have been his if he'd only behaved himself.

He came to work one day in the old beat-up car he did actually own. It supposedly belonged to a friend, that's what he told us. He was driving it to get repairs done after work that day. Trying to help a friend out. Guess it needed a bunch of repairs because he drove it for the next several weeks.

Curiosity must be a part of human nature. Or maybe some folks are just born to be investigators. Whichever, his boasting and loud mouth drew a lot of suspicious co-workers. Especially when he started driving that beat-up old car.

Someone knew someone that knew his girlfriend. Now ex-girlfriend. She spilled the beans, told them everything. He owned nothing but his old car. She was very rich and owned all of it. The cars, the house, plus the mini park! Even the clothes on his back! All of it! She loved him with all her heart. All he had to do was love and treat her right. She would have shared it all with him. Too bad though. Loving her and treating her right was too difficult for him to do. He was caught with another woman. She let him come in with nothing but that old car, and that's what he had when she kicked him out. Talk about humiliation and embarrassment. They rubbed it in his face every day at work. He was as quiet as a mouse the rest of the time he worked there. I felt sorry for him.

The point I was making to my wife was, "just because a

person boasts about what they possess doesn't mean they actually have it. If they do, it may not really be theirs. The lies will come back and bite them in the end." Still she wasn't completely convinced that her new friend might be a phony. She would not believe that a person who talked about their possessions like that could possibly not have them. It sounded too good to be false. She was having a green moment, like there was no wisdom in her at all. Only time would expose the truth.

Her new friend was as popular as ever. He had everything to do with the crowds that raided her store when he was in town. I worked there one day a week and barely got customers. Got a lot of turned up noses and evil looks though! Everyone he met seemed to like him. His appeal and enthusiasm kept them coming back. My wife made his day, and he made theirs.

"They're crazy about him!" she said.

He began spending big money at the store and at the surrounding businesses. Often he treated his new friends to lunch or dinner. Even the other shop owners were eating out of his hands. My wife informed me of everything that happened. I estimate that 95% of our conversations were about him. I got tired of hearing it. Wanted to push the mute button whenever his name was mentioned! It made me a bit jealous and trust me; it takes a lot to make me jealous. The fact is, they became best of friends in such a short time. Any husband would have felt some jealously. According to her, there was no need to be. It was all innocent. I'm sure she'd be jealous too if I had such a good female friend. I believe she would have acted a fool. She didn't consider that. Maybe future problems could be avoided if folks put themselves in the other person's shoes.

This guy was like a first-round-draft-pick, all the women wanted him and the fellows wanted to be his best bud. Nobody had anything negative to say about him. He was placed up high on a golden pedestal.

Since he came into the store, nothing was the same; at the store or at home. He became a major issue in just a matter of weeks.

"You need to be careful and stop trusting this guy," I told my wife.

"He's harmless, he won't hurt a fly," she claimed.

"There's other ways of doing harm other than the physical," I said.

I heard of people questioning her relationship with him. That brought on some serious concerns about this. At the beginning it seemed temporary. I realized he was here to stay and cause confusion. The warning signs were there, but some individuals are more hardheaded than others. Sadly, this group included my wife. Why would they not listen to the ones who truly love them? Why can't they see through the disguise of a trickster?

CHAPTER 3

The Past

WHAT WOULD PEOPLE do if they could go back in time? Would they change anything? Would we avoid the horrible mistakes that infected our lives with so much misery? Most of us would probably set ourselves up for riches and glory in the future. If we could go back, life would probably be perfect. Maybe that's why GOD won't allow it. Too bad for me. I can think of a thousand things to change that would make my life much-much better. Especially my involvement with certain people over the years. They were crabs in a bucket, pulling me down when I was almost free. Their misery loved my company. Whatever state they were in, they wanted me there too. Anyway, that's one of the things I'd definitely change. Some choices I would think twice about also. Unfortunately, these include my choice of mate.

Yes! I know! In any romantic relationship there will be bumps and bruises. But, shouldn't there be smooth sailing at the beginning? I mean, you're still just getting to know each other, right? You should be so excited, that there's no time for trouble. That wasn't the case with me and my wife when we started dating. We acquired many bumps and bruises within the first month. Can you see why I question my choice?

Not that it was completely her fault, or mine. So called family and friends contributed to these troubles too. My belief is; knowing what I know now, it may be a good idea to go your separate ways and abandon the relationship. When there are problems at the start of course. You'll be better off starting a new one with somebody else. Think about it as you go through some more of our history.

We were both young and immature when we first met. Only a year or two since graduating high school. The only thing on our minds was having fun. If you're old enough, you've been there. We were looking for something fun to do on that night I met my wife to be. My buddy was dating one of her relatives. She was having a small get-together with other family and friends. We sort of crashed the party, not knowing they were having it. My pal just wanted to see his girl. I didn't expect to meet anybody on that cold winter night. But one stood out from the rest.

She had the most beautiful face I had ever seen. Her sweet personality was second to none and her appearance rivaled that of a super model. She was outgoing and loved to speak her mind. My wife to be had all the qualities I wanted in a woman. Strangely though, I wasn't interested in her in that way at first. Didn't wanna get involved with her. Honestly, I never thought in a million years we'd end up together. We had so much fun and laughter that night, that we both thought we would be no more than friends. Besides, I was already seeking relationships with other women. Was trying to make-up my mind for which one I was going to date. But somewhere down the line something clicked with us. A bond developed between us which seemed unbreakable. My wife and I started dating and never looked backed.

Like stated before, we were immature. Everyone knows that a lack of maturity causes us to do unwise and childish things. Sometimes these things come back to haunt us later on. Particularly when you have the type of mate that remembers all your childish mishaps. Who's also slow to forgive and forget. Like mine was!

I did what most young men would do to impress a young lady they wanted to be with. I told small lies to make me bigger than I really was. Didn't take a moment to think she might actually find out the truth. Didn't expect her to react with so much fury either. After the whole truth was revealed, she made sure I'd never forget the lies. Year after year I was reminded of them. Even after years of being married to her. With a passion, I hated when we discussed them. Packing my things and leaving crossed my mind a few times. That was because she refused to ease up and let go. Can you see how this can affect a relationship?

Small lies in the past caused future mistrust. She would believe strangers before she believed me sometimes. It got pretty bad until she realized it was only a part of my plan to win her at the beginning. It's a part of being young. She also heard from friends whose mates did the exact same thing. Guess I should have thanked them. The pressure eased, but the fibs had already done enough damage. I believe those lies never stopped bothering her.

I uncovered another fact; the way relatives treat your new mate can have an impact on your relationship too. If it's positive treatment, then the impact will be positive. If not, then the opposite. We met each other's family at the beginning of our getting together. Hers embraced and treated me like one of their own. With my family though, it was a whole different story. Let me re-phrase that! With my female family members, it was a whole different story.

I think my mom never really had an issue with my future wife. She just allowed my sisters and others to greatly influence her. They treated my future wife as if she stole something from them. It's amazing she stayed with me for so many years after their first meeting. The things they did would have made any woman leave. So many foolish attempts to spoil any chances we had of having a life together. On one occasion, even I was caught up in one of their meaningless endeavors. I was naive and not thinking at the time. It all started when she stepped through my mother's front door.

"Hey Mom!" I said as I kissed her on the cheek. My little brother and sister were both there. They said their hellos and what's ups. They weren't expecting me to bring someone else. I introduced her as she walked in. They were very surprised.

Everyone except my sister said, "Hi!"

She eyeballed my future wife, rolled her eyes, and said to me, "so-and-so told me to tell you to call her." So-and so was someone in my past.

I could not believe my sister lied like that. She brought up the name of a woman in my past, and made it look as if I was still involved with her. I hadn't seen or spoken to this woman in two years. Matter of fact, we never got around to dating. We were only friends. I knew my sister was lying about calling her. Didn't know why she did it at first, but found out a few years later. I got a rude awakening. Thought everyone would be happy for me since this was my first time bringing a lady friend home to meet my folks. The first time I'd ever been this serious about a woman.

"Why would I call her?" I asked in retaliation. I was hoping to keep my future wife from becoming more upset than my sister had already made her. In an attempt to show her I had no interest in other women, and to shut my sister up, I said, "I'm with the lady I wanna be with right now! Besides, I haven't spoken to that girl in years! I got no reason to call her!"

Guess my sis wasn't looking for a response like that. Now both of them were upset. My wife-to-be cooled down after a while and was back to her normal self. She even stopped giving me mean stares. She had nice, friendly conversations with my mom and brother. As for my sister, I might have witnessed the nastiest attitude that a human being could ever have. There was a look on her face that could have repelled a grizzly bear. That look never left her face. I never saw her that way before.

My future wife tried to befriend her as me and mom talked. She bent over backwards to be her friend. I had trouble listening to my mom because my attention was focused on my sister's attitude. The sound of her voice proved she wasn't thrilled about my future wife at all. After a while, it mellowed out, but still there was no thrill. The conversation improved though the look was still there. Maybe she was having a horrible day and needed someone to take it out on, I thought.

I forced myself to focus back on my mom. We stayed there for about four or five hours. Most of the discussions were about the general stuff. You know, family and friends. Time after time I would glance over at my sister. She was speaking with that same look on her face. I just couldn't figure it out. We were the closest of all our siblings. We always supported each other no matter what. Why was she not happy for me this time? Her behavior on that day caused me to be disappointed in her for the first time.

Mom seemed ok with my new girlfriend. But at the end of our visit, only my brother congratulated me on my new found love. We left once we said our goodbyes. I must admit, I was not satisfied with that visit. Not even a little bit. You know how it feels when you expect praises from relatives, but all you get is a, "you could have done better!" With the exception of my little brother, that's what I was feeling from them. I remember how bad I felt for my girl also. She was completely quiet for the first half of our trip home. Didn't know what to say so I kept my mouth shut too. Actually, I was hoping it stayed that way. Didn't feel like arguing. I was in a bad mood and could tell she was still somewhat upset. All it took was a spark to set things off.

The halfway point was drawing near. It was late night and drowsiness started kicking in. Then the silence was finally broken. Thankfully though, there was no serious argument. Only a brief exchange of what happened earlier.

"So what's your sister's problem?" she asked.

"Maybe she was having a bad day," I responded. "You know how it is."

"She sure has a mean and nasty way of showing it. Did you see how she treated me? What was her plan? Wait for someone like me to come over so she could release her anger."

Remember what I stated earlier about being caught up in one of my family's senseless efforts to hurt my relationship? Well, right there is when it started.

I became defensive and raised my voice slightly. "Look! You don't know my sister! This is your first time meeting her! She's not like that!"

"Why are you raising your voice?" she asked. "I just wanna know what's going on. That's all."

"I don't know," I said in a lower voice. "You're right. I shouldn't have raised my voice at you. It's not your fault and she upset me too. I never saw my sister like this before. Something must be bothering her."

"Well, I wanna talk to her again to get to know her better."

"You will," I said. "I'm gonna call her tomorrow to see what's the problem."

"All right. Sounds good."

We discussed other things the rest of the way. We made it home and turned in. The next day I called my little sister as promised. Man do I wish I hadn't! What I did afterwards caused tremendous grief between my wife-to-be and I. Just like the small lies I told at the beginning, my next slip-up was re-kindled in our marriage for many years to come. It caused many fights.

I asked my sister what was wrong. This is what she told me. "Your new girlfriend has a serious problem! She had an attitude with me first! She's stuck up and thinks she's better than us! I don't like her!"

That lie about my girl's attitude and personality was told to many of my female relatives. They believed every word of it. As for me, I entered the state of denial. I was blinded. I would not believe my closest sibling would lie like that. It just couldn't sink into my brain. I knew my future wife and that she didn't carry herself that way. All she wanted was to be at peace with everyone and help all she could. Like an idiot though, I chose my sister's side. It caused me to confront my future wife. We argued about it and ended the relationship. We were back to-gether within a week. That fight continued for a while and I can't count how many times we split up. Nevertheless, we al-ways got back together for some reason.

Remember the choices I wish I'd thought twice about. I would make that first breakup permanent if I could go back in time. A lot of pain and sorrow could have been avoided. But it wasn't. I eventually sided with my future wife. The damage was already done though. I found out that my sister told multiple lies. They had spread like wildfires before getting back to me. She had my family brainwashed to the point that I too was treated like an enemy. If possible, they would have chewed off my head if I'd said anything negative about my little sis. I never looked at or thought of her in the same way ever again. I was so hurt.

I stayed away from them for a while. My wife-to-be never forgave me for this no matter how many apologies she received. Even throughout our marriage. I know that for a fact. Whenever we talked about it, she expressed how it hurt her and then burst into tears. All my efforts to comfort her were always rejected. Imagine the negative effect this had on our relationship.

Three years had passed before I saw my sister again. I'd been hearing horror stories about her. How she interfered with other male relatives' marriages and relationships. They included two of my brothers' marriages in which one ended in divorce. I was told she influenced it a lot. She even recruited some of my female cousins who obviously shared her motives. Nobody knew why they did it, just thought they were insane.

She had her own family when we met up. A husband and two children. We were surprised at how she treated us. She was very nice and respectable. Especially toward my wife, whom I had been married to then for four years. We sat and talked for hours. Then out of the blue it happened. My wife asked the question.

"Why did you treat me so bad when we first met? Why so many lies?"

"Girl, I was being childish and stupid," my sister responded. "I was jealous and felt my brother was being taken from us."

I wanted to respond to that but held my tongue. I wanted to ask my sister if she felt that way when she stuck her nose in my brothers' marriages. I thought she was full of it. I still love her, just can't trust her.

Now, let's talk about some grief dealt to me in the past. Years ago, I realized I was wrong for defending my sister. I regretted it very much. That might have bothered my wife more than any other mischief I did in the past. She too did something that bothered me greatly. It started shortly after we began dating. I still can't figure out why she thought it was ok. Just like me siding with my sister was foul to her, what she did was foul to me. Both our actions caused a negative effect. The main difference, I think, was she showed no remorse for her actions.

Wanna know what she did? She took the liberty of congregating with multiple male friends. Well, so called male friends. A few were my cousins whom she seemed to care more about than me. I believe every man shares my feelings about this. I didn't want my woman hanging out with male buddies. They were just looking for an opportunity to get her in the bed. She actually thought they only wanted to be her friends.

"We're just friends," she said. "I'd rather hang out with men anyway. Women are too jealous."

"Men get jealous too," I said. "But you don't see me hanging out with women because of that. Do you?"

I told her I didn't like it, of course she didn't listen. The more I showed my disapproval of it, the more she seemed to want to do it. They hung out for hours at a time. It got worse as my patience grew thinner. Only I owned a car during the time we were dating. She began using it while I was at my job working hard. She ran errands and took care of other important matters for me. She started keeping my car almost every day of the work week. I didn't mind because I never left work until the end of the day. Besides, she was doing things for her parents too. Well, at first she was!

Something happened in her mind once my work days got longer. I started working irregular overtime hours. It got to where I didn't know when I was getting off each day. Guess she saw that as a good chance to spend more time with her so called buddies. Back then I was young and naive, remember? I knew she was hanging out with them, but didn't know exactly how long and how often. She got use to picking me up late because of the extreme overtime hours. I called her when it was time to be picked up. Five or ten minutes later, I'd be in my car on the way home.

On one particular Friday, the unexpected happened. I got off work at the normal time. I couldn't wait to call and surprise her. Guess who got the big surprise. I called, and called, and called, but could not get in touch with her. Cell phones were not that popular back then with only a few folks owning them. No chance of reaching her that way. I was calling from an outside phone booth. Nobody had seen her since early that morning after I was dropped off. I spent the next ten hours trying to reach her from work. There was no one around who could give me a ride home. The location of my job made walking too far and dangerous. The fact that it was late night didn't help the situation either.

I became very concerned, which turned into anger as she finally pulled up. One of her so called friends was sitting in the passenger seat. I thought about kicking him out of my car and leaving him there. I should have, but I didn't. She started apologizing soon as I got in. I said nothing all the way home. She dropped him off and what she said next was the last straw with those male friends.

"I'm sorry, the car broke down," she said. "We couldn't get it started."

I wanted to know who "we" were. She openly told me everything. She had been joy riding all day long with her so called friends in my car. In my car! Just her and a bunch of no good low lives, including my cousins. Then the car broke down. She brought one guy with her, a proclaimed mechanic, in case there was another breakdown. Do you think I thanked him? Not at all! He was blessed that I didn't punch him out. This joy riding happened on other days too. Riding around, behaving like teenagers who took their parents' car without them knowing it. She was in a car full of men. Had they been women or relatives of hers, I don't think I would have been as angry. She was given an ultimatum. It was me or them. Her decision was silent. She chose me but never said it. As far as I know, that was the last time she hung out with all male friends. I never got an apology.

A few months went by and the bumps and bruises kept on coming. There was another episode concerning a so called male friend of hers. It involved one of my cousins I mentioned before. Of all the events of her showing too much concern for other men, this one took the cake. I despised this one most of all. Not just because my cousin was involved, but she showed little regard for me. I never got an apology for that either.

We weren't living together at the time this took place; weren't married yet. She would come over to my place and spend a night or two sometimes. During that time also, my cousin was having some major problems. I was very fond of him and wanted to help out. He needed a place to stay, so he lived with me for a while. My future wife had grown fond of him too. That was way before I let him move in however. She actually met him before meeting me. They've always conversed. What I'm trying to say is, I thought it was ok for her to come over while he was there. That was until I discovered he wanted more than just her friendship. I overheard him talking about it to one of his pals. I thought it was very lowdown and dirty of him. You help somebody out, and this is how they repay you. That was one of my life lessons of how males and females can't be friends if one is interested in the other. I was interested also. Interested in what would happen. I tested her and kept quiet about my cousin for a while.

As you may have guessed, my fondness for him dissipated. Would you care for someone who's been deceiving you for so long? He was thought to be an angel, but turned out to be a con-man. I found out later that all his problems were not true. His brother told me what was going on. That's a whole other story within itself. He fooled me good, she was totally fooled though. She almost worshipped the ground he walked on. I thought it had gone on long enough.

"My cousin means you no good at all," I told her. "He's got you fooled just like he had me."

"What are you talking about now?" she asked.

"I heard him talking to that friend of his. He's got big plans for you and him after some party they're having. You got your invitation yet?"

"Look! He's not like that," she said, "he's too nice and doesn't think like that. Even if he did, why are you so worried? I wouldn't dare, he's not even close to my type!"

"Still, I don't want you here with him alone."

She agreed to that although she didn't believe what I said about him. Felt I was being jealous for some reason. She thought he was the nicest person she had ever met. He had her total respect while I was totally disrespected by her. That's what really upset me. Especially on one unusually cool day in July. I came home from work and she was asleep on the sofa. The air conditioner was blasting and the place felt like a refrigerator. I wanted to take a shower and not get sick during the process. So I shut off the ac. That lit a fuse. She awoke and started screaming at me.

"Did I tell you to turn the ac off? Turn it back on and don't turn it off again!"

"What!" I said. "I'm about to take a shower and it's freezing in here!"

"I don't care!" she said. "It feels hot to me and I want the air on!"

I didn't feel like arguing, so I nearly froze to death taking my shower. Not long after I got dressed, he walked in. She sprang up and greeted him with a big "hello"! Like he was royalty or something. He went into his room for a moment. He came out and asked if we needed to use the bathroom. He wanted to take a shower. We said no and he stepped into the bathroom. What my future wife did next almost got her kicked out of my place and out of my life permanently. She jumped up and hurried to the thermostat.

She shut off the ac and told my cousin, "I'm gonna turn this off so you won't get sick."

I could feel anger in every cell of my body. However, I kept my cool. I wanted to be calm when I asked her why.

"Why did you do that?" I asked softly.

"Do what?"

"You turned the air off for him. You wanted to cut my throat when I did it. Why?"

"Stop being silly," she said with a smirk on her face." Why would I do that?"

I asked again, but she claimed she didn't remember getting mad at me for shutting it off. Of course I didn't believe her. It happened less than an hour earlier. That was another mystery to me. Never knew the exact reason, only had an idea why she did it. I kicked him out soon after. Not just because of this ordeal with my woman, mainly because he lied about the hardship he was going through. She was mad at me for a while and said I was wrong for treating him that way. Then she found out later what I said about him was true. She couldn't stand him and thought he was the supreme jerk.

Our relationship began to stabilize during the two years we dated. We got married although all the craziness hadn't been put behind us. I couldn't imagine myself being without her. We were willing to deal with any problems or issues that came our way. Even if it was Satan himself tempting us with his wicked devices, including people.

When people other than our spouses hit on or flirt with us, it makes us feel good. This lets us know we still have it and it's a confidence booster. I'm sure it happens or has happened to everyone that's been in a relationship. It's ok as long as we don't yield to any temptation. It's a good feeling, but I feel we shouldn't tell our mates when it happens. That'll cut down on issues such as jealousy.

Now, what part did Satan play when it happened to us? He knows exactly what we like and enjoy even before he approaches us. My wife loved when other men flirted with her. I know because she told me whenever it happened. She would have the biggest smile on her face and she seemed to be glowing. I really didn't have any issues with that. The problem was her rubbing it in my face whenever it happened.

Another problem was those guys who took flirting too far. Maybe they could see how she enjoyed it and figured they had a chance with her. She was offered money, houses, and cars. This became a frequent thing and I was informed by her each time it happened. I became jealous and started telling her about the women that hit on me. There was an unofficial competition between us, who would get the most flirts. She was beating me 10 to 1 and continued rubbing it in. I got so tired of her boasting that I almost yielded to temptation myself. That would have out done all the flirting she received.

Now can you see what Satan's role was? He was there in the beginning to set us up to fall. Thankfully though, it wasn't our time yet. This was just another bump or bruise in our union.

Like any other couple, we did and said things in the past to hurt each other. Why we do it, I don't know. Guess it's a part of life. These things must be forgiven if we are to have a healthy relationship. Both sides must understand that immature mistakes will be made as you grow together. If one side isn't willing to do that, then the relationship will remain in jeopardy. In that case, wouldn't it be best to examine our choice of mate before making any serious commitments; if we hadn't already made them. Too bad for me! I am living proof that the past can dictate future outcomes of marriages or relationships. For better or for worse!

CHAPTER 4

Playing Games

THEN WE WERE at the beginning of our most difficult period. I truly believe my wife never meant for things to happen the way they did. I believe her feelings got caught up and the situation caused her to improvise as things worsen. She started lying compulsively; mainly to me and to her mom about her whereabouts. Didn't even have to ask where she was each day. She called and let me know every two or three hours; lying of course. I trusted her and thought nothing of it at the time. There was no need to call around looking for her. Most of the time, she said she was out with her mom doing things. And with certain friends whom I had no way of contacting even if I wanted to ask questions about her. She became an expert at covering all her mischievous tracks. But all things must come to light.

One day, I visited her store a few hours before closing time. Hadn't been there in weeks. To my surprise, she had closed up already. It was around one o'clock in the afternoon. Normally, she'd call and let me know whether she was closing early or late. Maybe she had something very important to do or some business meeting to attend. It didn't bother me at all. Not until one of her regular customers showed up.

"Man, she closed early again," he said. "I was hoping I could get some of those chocolate bars she sells out of all the time. This is the only time I'm able to drop in, but she's been closed for the last four days."

"Is that so?" I asked.

I remember this particular customer. He'd come in every other day and buy those chocolate bars while I was working the store. He was an older fellow, well spoken and full of gray. He seemed very intelligent, but had a problem remembering certain faces. He didn't remember mine or that the owner was my wife. He forgot she was married at all. He gave me an earful of information about her and the friend she was keeping company with. It was the same guy she promised to cut loose.

"Yes indeed," he answered, "this must be some special friend of hers. He's always here, helping her in the store and stuff. He's a good young man, handsome too. He takes her out to lunch all the time, he buys her things. Shoot, we might be hearing wedding bells soon!"

I sat and listen to him go on and on about them. I even played into it just to get names of places where they hung out. Not to go there and start trouble, but so I could confront her about it.

I claimed, "I need a nice place to take my ole lady. What's the name of some of these spots he takes her to?"

He told me everything I needed to know. Their midday meetings had been going on for weeks; almost as soon as I stopped working in the store. I was so angry I thought I felt my brain scorching. Couldn't wait to get home and tell her what I knew about them. I burned rubber off my tires as I raced off the parking lot. I'm not bragging, but I think I'm an excellent driver. Always driving the speed limit and following all the rules. But on that particular day, I disregarded everything. I had no speed limit. I can't count how many wrecks I could have been involved in. It's amazing I didn't get arrested that day. It's amazing nobody died. I finally got home and the streets were relieved. She called as soon as I stepped through the front door.

"Hey baby!" she said. "I'm closing up a little late tonight so don't wait up for me. Ok!"

"All right," I said like there was no problem.

Thankfully, my children were at their grandmother's for the night. They did not need to hear the argument that was getting ready to erupt. It wouldn't be good for them. I waited and thought about how I would come at her. She showed up around ten that night. That was later than she had been coming home the last few weeks. I was in the bed pretending to be asleep. She took a shower and readied herself for bed. As she lied down, I spoke up.

"So how was your day?" I asked.

"Oh, I didn't mean to wake you baby."

"You didn't. How was your day?"

"I had to stay open longer, but it was nothing special."

My plans were to remain calm and chat a while longer, but that lie made it too hard.

"So did you and your boyfriend have a good time today?"

Then there was a suspenseful fifteen seconds of silence. Guess she was startled and had trouble finding something to say.

"What are you talking about now?" she asked nervously as she giggled slightly.

Yeah! She was very concerned. I never heard her voice so shaky before. I got up and turned on the light so we could see each other's face.

"What are you doing?" she asked.

"Where were you around one o'clock today?"

"Working in the store!"

"I was there, I didn't see you!" I yelled.

Ain't it strange how people react when they know they've been busted? They can see that you know what's going on, but they deny it anyway. Do they think they can convince you contrary to what you already know?

"I was there, you weren't looking hard enough!" she claimed.

"Stop lying! The door was locked and the 'CLOSED' sign was in the window! You think I'm stupid?"

"I was there. You should have looked around for me!"

"Where were you the last four days when you closed early?"

She paused and had that look on her face. You know, the look that says, "How did he know that?"

"Oh yeah! I know about the restaurants you two eat at and the places where he takes you on shopping sprees! Buy you anything special today?"

I named all the restaurants and stores, and the days when they were seen there. You would have thought she had seen a ghost. Some people think they could never be caught. She became fire hot mad knowing she was indeed catchable.

"Can we talk about something else?" she asked with a loud and angry voice.

"No!" I yelled back. "Let's talk about this!"

"Well, you can talk to yourself about it! I'll be at my mom's!" she yelled.

"You did wrong, but you're the one that's leaving! I just want you to tell me the truth!"

She didn't say another word. She grabbed some of her things and headed for the door. I attempted to stop her by grabbing her arm, but she gave me a look that would make a pit bull let go. I loved my wife and wanted her to stay so this could be sorted out. But for some reason, I had to let her leave that night. Now that I think about it, things probably would have gotten way out of control if she had stayed. I was extremely angry. She said she stopped dealing with this guy. Most of my anger was kindled because she was lying about it. Looking me in my eyes and telling so many lies. I felt like going ballistic. I didn't because I knew at the time she went no further than going out with him.

I tried calling and was told she didn't wanna talk to anybody at the time. I respected her wishes and decided to wait it out. Still I prayed she would call and tell me everything. It would have made me feel a lot better. The next morning my prayer was answered. Thankfully, it was more than what I asked for. She called to tell me she wanted to talk face to face. Thirty minutes later, we were in our living room doing just that.

"Hey," she greeted.

"Hey," I replied.

She grabbed me around my mid-section as she spoke, "I am so sorry for not being honest with you. Please forgive me!"

I said nothing; however, I had already forgiven her. She explained that they were still friends. She did actually tell him not to bother her anymore, but she couldn't stop him from coming around. He'd come in and talk to her, but showed no more interest in the way he did before.

"Yes, we went out to eat a few times, and he also took the other shop owners out. I went shopping and he offered to pay for whatever I was buying. I allowed him to pay the first time he asked to. I paid all the other times cause I didn't feel right letting him do it. That's the type of person he is. He loves to give."

"But why did you get so upset when you found out I knew?" I asked.

"Because I really didn't want you to know we were still friends. I knew how angry you would get. I felt bad cause I told you I would break all ties with him but didn't. I lied to you and you had to find out through someone else. Do you know how that made me feel? Pretty low. But believe me, this is all innocent."

She said she enjoyed being friends with him and I had absolutely nothing to worry about. Easy for her to say! I remembered at one time how very much interested he was in her. I explained for about an hour how much I was against this friendship of hers. Yet, I stayed out of the way.

Time had passed and things were actually going good. No big problems arose because of her friend and we were spending a lot of time together. Then her girlfriends started talking.

The Bible says that all sorts of animals have been tamed. All kinds of wild beasts. But the tongue can never be tamed. They started talking and filling her head with poison. Most of them never wanted to see us together anyway. That's been proven time after time. Our relationship always seemed to be going better than theirs. They were delighted to hear about this guy.

"People are so nosey!" she said to me one day. "They all keep asking me about this man."

She appeared to be full of joy when she told me that. Being the center of attention always seemed to fulfill something in my wife. So I understood where the joy came from. What I couldn't understand is why people call themselves your friend but behave like your adversary. From what I was told, one day they were discussing normal female buddy stuff. Then out of the blue, one of her pals brought his name up. They wanted to know everything about him. How she met him and what they did whenever they hung out together. My wife was an open book, being the center of attention. Her buddies were enlightened from the beginning to the present state of their friendship. She even told them how much I objected to this new friend of hers.

"I thought about cutting him loose for good," my wife told them.

"Girl," one of them replied, "this man is good looking, he's got money, and you know he's got a thing for you. Why do you think he keeps on coming around? And you wanna cut him loose! Are you crazy? He can buy you whatever you want. I think you should keep him around. You know, just in case."

"Just in case what?" my wife asked.

"You know. In case things don't work with you and your husband."

I couldn't believe my wife's attitude as she told me about this conversation with them. She acted as if it were a joke. She didn't take it serious at all when I told her she should cut those friends loose too. She giggled about it and brushed me off.

"GOD sent this guy to you for a reason," another friend told her.

When I heard that, I asked my wife, "How much alcohol did your friend drink before she said that?"

I truly thought she was high on something. Why would GOD send someone to cause trouble in a marriage? Her friends made a lot of dumb comments that were uncalled for. I wanted to know what they were up to. What was their purpose for bringing this issue up whenever they got together? I found out soon enough.

My wife had a relative, whom I loved and had the utmost

respect for. This person helped me in many ways and always gave excellent advice.

But I was hurt and cut deep when this individual told my wife, "you should stay with your husband for now, and also keep this guy around to see what he's all about."

Why was this and all the other comments made to my wife? This question had a simple answer and I kept missing it for some reason. It didn't take a lot of intelligence to figure it out either. It was all because of what my wife was saying to them first. I felt like a complete idiot. I found out she was telling them about all the problems we were having at home. They were told we were probably not gonna make it much longer. And all she did was boast about this guy. How he buys her things and the way he treats her. The way he talks to her. And when this relative of hers said she should keep him around, the bottom fell out of our life. It's like she took it as an ok to be with this fellow. My children and I didn't seem to matter anymore. She was gonna see this man with or without my consent. She started staying out very late and I knew exactly why.

What was I to do? What any husband who loved his wife would have done. I was determined to be with her and break all ties she had with him. It was about time I got physical. As I was driving up to the store to beat him up, I thought about how many bones to break and which order to do it in. He was going to the emergency room that night. When I pulled into the parking lot, she was standing out by the curb. Guess she could feel what I was about to do.

"He left already," she said. "You promised you wouldn't do this! You're only gonna make things worse!"

We got into my car and argued about him for about an hour. It was good that he wasn't there. I would still be in prison until this day for doing what I'd planned to do to him. It wouldn't have been pretty. We eventually cooled down and went home to talk some more.

"I'm sorry for the way things have happened," she said. "I didn't mean for any more trouble. I only wanna be his friend."

"So why spread our business and talk to your friends about him?" I asked.

"I don't know why I did it, but I'm ending it right now."

I didn't know whether to believe her or not. She really seemed sincere this time and made me promise again not to approach him concerning this. She would take care of everything and we would be together. So I gave her another chance.

If anyone ever said, "love blinds us," they were right. But I could only blame myself for the hardship I was about to face. I stopped blaming my wife when I realized she wasn't her normal self as these things took place. It took a while though. Whatever got in her became a part of her life. It caused her to do things I've never seen before. The trickery she used was on a whole other level. Whenever there was an opportunity, she tried to make me look bad.

It started when I was laid off from my job. I was diligently seeking for employment anywhere I could find it. From sun up til sun down I was either putting in an application somewhere, or faxing and emailing resumes. I was determined to get a job, but times were tough. For every twenty or thirty jobs applied for, one responded; and they were all negative responses. My wife knew I loved to work and couldn't stand being without a job. She told me something one day that surprised me. Once again, couldn't understand why, at first.

"Baby," she said, "why don't you just forget about a job and take a break for a while? Get your unemployment. It'll help out for the time being. Remember I still got the store."

It took some time, but she finally convinced me to do it. I figured a couple of months off would give me time to bond more with my children and concentrate on ironing our problems out. It seemed to be working for the first month. Then I started hearing things she had been saying about me. She told people I had become very lazy since my lay off. Supposedly, I was sitting around enjoying unemployment checks and didn't care about working anymore. Wasn't lifting a finger to find another job! She actually told people that lie. When I confronted her about it, she couldn't recall suggesting that I should take a break for a while. In just a short time, she had convinced herself that her husband was a lazy nobody. Her attitude became, "I'M RIGHT NO MATTER WHAT", in the blink of an eye. Each time we argued about it, she stormed out of the house and wouldn't be seen again until the next day. She had a plan, and all of this was the first part of it.

Remember when she made me promise not to start any trouble with this guy? Well, people said I was a wimp because I wouldn't fight for her. They said I was less than a man and there was no defense of me on her part. She didn't mention to them that she had me promise I wouldn't do anything. She forgot that also. She was told, "If he don't fight for you, apparently he don't want you! If I were you, I would date this guy since your husband don't care anyway!" That was all she needed to hear. The children and I didn't matter anymore. I knew because she said it when we argued.

She knew I was gonna break that promise. She pulled all types of strings to keep me from getting to this guy. I would let her leave for work each day. An hour later after driving the children to school, I would arrive at the store and look for him. Unfortunately, she was very good at covering her tracks. It took a while for me to either find them together or catch him alone. One day, I figured it out. Knew exactly how to do it the next time! I remember laughing as I pictured myself stomping him while he was laid out on the ground. I could hear her telling me to stop it. Man; that really felt good!

The next day when she left, I waited only ten minutes then followed her. I was so pumped up about hurting this guy that, I didn't even bother taking my children to school. They were right there with me. My mind couldn't have been operating correctly. There was a chance that they were going to see my violent side. I had them stay in the car as I went inside. As I walked through the door, I noticed she wasn't there. It was only him and a customer.

"Hey!" I said.

He turned and shock filled his face. Wasn't expecting me I guess.

"Hey," he said as he tried to shake my hand. Of course that wasn't gonna happen.

"Where's my wife? Why isn't she here?" I asked with a rough voice.

He seemed surprised to see me, but he was comfortable in my presence. Not nervous at all. Something was wrong with this picture. He should have felt some form of discomfort even if he thought he could take me; just for the fact I was her husband. He was completely relaxed.

"She stepped out for a minute," he said.

He brought me into the conversation he was having with the customer. For some reason, I couldn't allow myself to punch him. There was something my wife wasn't telling me. Looking into his face while he talked, made me realized that. I also felt she wasn't being truthful to him about everything. I was compelled to start asking questions. She came back before I could get answers from him.

"What are you doing? Come here!" she yelled as she grabbed my arm and pulled me out of the store.

She went into a rage, yelling and cursing at me. There was a big crowd around and they all had their eyes on us. I was frozen and couldn't say a word. Nobody I loved ever talked to me like that before. I've been yelled at and cursed out many times, but not like this. What was I to do? I walked away as one of her relatives tried to calm her down. My eyes were full of tears by the time I reached my car. I tried my best to hide it from my children. They knew something was wrong though. We sat there as I attempted to convince myself, "that didn't just happen!" My wife came to the car a few minutes later, got in, and just stared at me for a while.

"Why did you come here today?" she asked. "You brought the kids too! What were you trying to do?"

I didn't say anything; didn't even look at her. Just sat there with no words for her. Then she kissed me on the cheek.

"I'm sorry," she said, "I'll talk to you when I get home." She went back into the store.

We sat for about ten more minutes without a sound. My mind was completely blank.

"When are we going home?" my son asked.

I never answered back. Just sat and stared through the windshield. After a while, I came to myself and we headed home. My thoughts were all crossed up. I tried to figure this out but other things popped into my mind. I got a little scared because it seemed my life was flashing before my eyes. I had to pull over for a moment. I could hear my children talking to me, but their voices kept tuning in and out. I thought I was losing it. We got home and nothing changed. I was out of it. I sat down to think but couldn't. A giant, blank white wall was all I could see. I sat there in some kind of trance.

Don't know how, but I fell asleep. It was late night by the time I awoke. The children were asleep and I was stunned that my wife was there. She was sitting beside me, waiting for me to wake up I guess. Still didn't want to say anything to her. She began speaking.

"I know you are very, very upset with me," she said. "Anybody would be. I wanna explain what's going on. Will you hear me out?"

There was a moment of silence.

"Ok, let's hear it," I said.

"I know I've lied to you, and did a lot of things that wounded you in the last few months. I don't know why I'm doing this. Believe me when I say it bothers me more than anything else. You know me, and this is not me. I lied to you and him too."

Those words made me look at her. I didn't say anything but she knew I wanted to know.

"Yeah, I lied to him too. He told me from the start, he didn't wanna come between my marriage. He was gonna stop bothering me when I told him to. But, I really didn't want him to stop. I told him my marriage was on the rocks and we were separated. I said you didn't want me anymore. I wanted him to keep pursuing me. I guess I got caught up in the excitement. I promise you I wanna end this. GOD knows I wanna do what's right."

Well, that explained why he was so calm earlier. I would have gotten physical with him for no reason. My wife was the guilty one in this. She spent the rest of that night apologizing and trying to convince me she would do right by me. I believed her slightly, but half the trust was already gone. She apologized every day for a whole week hoping to clear up my mind. Things got better after she asked me to work in the store with her again. I assumed he was told not to bother her anymore. We arrived and left together every day. He was nowhere to be found.

Life was back in order and our marriage was on the right track. Then I got an unusual phone call one morning while my wife was out shopping with her mom. The person calling was that crazy sister of mine. Hadn't heard from her for about a year! She needed to talk to me. After going through all that mess during those past few months, nothing anyone said should have been able to startle me. What my sister told me went well beyond startling.

"What's happening with your wife?" she asked.

She went on to tell me what was told to her. Carelessly, my wife was talking to my cousin's wife, a well-known blabber mouth. They were thought to be pretty close; not close enough I'd say! She told members of my family everything my wife said to her about our marriage. Apparently, I wasn't compatible with her anymore and she had a new man in her life.

My relatives started ringing my phone off the hook, but I was too embarrassed to talk to them. I knew my sister was telling the truth. There's no way they could have known about our situation unless my wife was giving them the info. She denied it of course. She said they always hated her and didn't want to see us together. She broke all ties with my cousin's wife. Who could blame her?

I was again overwhelmed with concern. What was happening to my wife and my marriage? Exactly how far were we from the end? Close, but more mess was on the way.

She started using trickery again when we attended church one Sunday. My wife was a member of the encouragement committee. At certain times of the month, they would present gifts and awards to individuals to encourage and inspire them. On that particular Sunday, she did something strange. After the presentation, she asked me to stand up. Some folks there didn't know who I was so she decided to introduce me.

"This is my husband!" she said as the crowd applauded. "I know I'm hard to get along with and I hope he don't kick me out of the house!"

She got a mixture of laughter and "uh oh's". I could hear people whispering, "I wander what's happening in their home."

Once again, I needed understanding. Why get in front of a large crowd and say something like that? Why? I'll tell you why! Because it was something she could use against me to help justify what she was getting ready to do.

CHAPTER 5

Separation

AS WE WENT on with our troubled marriage, separation became a big issue. It was discussed off and on each and every day. She wanted to do it because she thought it would make our marriage better. Not me, I was always against it. I felt it would bring nothing but more serious trouble. Not saying it wouldn't work for some people. For example; one of my friend's parents were separated for nearly twenty years. They split up, did their thing, and never got divorced. When I last saw them, they were back together and looked happier than ever. But from what I've seen in my lifetime, most separations end up as something permanent. That's what frightened me. I loved my wife very much and couldn't imagine being away from her. Too bad she wasn't thinking the same way. She flooded my ears with talk of separating. I told her it would be a big mistake and would open up doors for other problems. Other people told her the exact same thing. She refused to listen and kept bugging me about it. Then came the begging! She actually begged to be separated from me. She could have left on her own but for some reason; I had to agree to it.

"No, I won't do it!" I said. "Why do you want this so bad? You wanna be with that guy?"

"No, you know he's gone for good! I just wanna make this marriage better. Time apart would make us want each other more. Remember when your job use to send you away for so long? Remember how it felt when we saw each other when you got back? I wanna feel that again."

Still I rejected, but said I would think about it. It bothered me every time it crossed my mind. Should I do it? Yes and no played tug-a-war with my brain. I thought about all the positive and negative things that could happen. The negative outweighed the positive at least three to one. I sought the opinions of others. Some said it would help, others said the opposite. I remained in the state of undecided, but my wife gradually helped me find my way out of it. She started arguments about it every day. We would quarrel about separating for hours until she left. She'd go to her mom's and call when she got there. We'd argue some more until she was ready to come home and go to sleep. I got tired of it and finally gave in. We would separate, but there was a stipulation. We had to get marriage counseling from our pastor and she had to take care of the children on certain days of the week. She happily agreed to it.

Next, she wanted me to do something else that was strange.

"Hey, can you call Mom and let her know what we're doing? And when you do, ask if I could stay with her for a while."

"It's your mother!" I said. "You call her yourself!"

"Please!" she begged.

"Why do you want me to do it?"

"Because she would know that we're serious if you do it," she claimed.

It didn't seem right to me, so I refused. Once again, she had something to beg for. For the rest of that day, all I heard from her was, "please!" She didn't give me a break. She was determined that I would be the one to make the call.

I couldn't tell if she was playing another game or not. She seemed to be sincere about working things out with me. Besides, that guy was out of our life for good. I thought!

I gave in once I couldn't endure anymore begging. I made the call and her mom was also curious of why she didn't do it herself. She didn't think separating was a good idea either, but said it was our choice.

My wife started packing immediately after getting the ok

from her mom. We discussed a timeline for ending the separation and a date to get counseled. We called that same day to make an appointment for counseling, but disagreed about the timeline. She wanted to come back after six months; I wanted her back no later than two. Ultimately, we never did agree on one. I was hoping things would get better sooner than we both thought they might.

We were living in separation by the end of the day. Never thought that day would come for us. No, not for me and my wife! It just couldn't happen with us. Reality sunk in as I watched her walk out the door. The sky was sunny, but this was one of the darkest days of my life. My children's reaction, to her hugging them and walking out with her things, made me feel much, much worse. Their faces were painted with confusion. I wanted to explain what was happening, but couldn't find the appropriate words. Plus, I was afraid of the impact it would have on them at that time. We watched her drive off without a care in the world.

Some days went by and we waited for her return to do the things she agreed upon. She didn't show up on the day she was scheduled to get the kids. That prevented me from doing some very important chores. When I called and asked what happened, she said she was busy and would get them the next day. Did she show up the next day? Of course not! I tried contacting her for the next few days, but she was nowhere to be found. I avoided going to look for her because I didn't want to take the chance of upsetting her. So we just waited for her. The patience was killing me. She finally showed up two weeks later. She walked in like everything was fine.

"I was very busy doing things at church and for my mom," was her excuse.

She stayed for an hour or two, and was off again. Like that was ok with us! I really didn't know what to do. I hoped being calm and not worrying would cause things to work out. How wrong was I! She made it a habit to show her face weeks at a time. She became like a stranger. One day, she came in and tried to hug my daughter. My little girl refused and backed away. I could see that she was afraid too. My wife laughed about it, and I wanted to cry. That's when I started asking when was she coming home. She kept saying she's not ready and I should enjoy my freedom from her at the moment. Then she started staying away longer and longer. My patience dispersed and worry took control of me. I called her constantly and left message after message. My plan was that she'd get tired of it and contact me. It worked, but man it wasn't pleasant!

"Will you please stop calling me!" she yelled.

"Why are you yelling?" I asked. "I just wanna talk to you."

"I told you I've been very busy and I don't need you pressuring me!"

That started a big argument; which became a daily event. Yes, she began answering every day after I'd make so many calls to her. I didn't care if we argued, just wanted to hear her voice. We argued about everything we could think of. The fights ended whenever I brought that guy's name up. She would hang up and not answer again. The fights went on for about a month, and then things got calm again.

Next came the day of our marriage counseling session. We had a number of discussions about it as it drew closer. Even joked and laughed about some things. It had been a while since we'd been able to get along like that. She said she wanted to do something with me and the children the day before our appointment. I was excited and knew things were starting to fall back into place. I told my children and they were more excited than me. We prepared ourselves and waited for her all day long. She was to meet us at the house at a certain time so we could ride out together. That time came and passed. She never showed up. It frustrated me mostly because the children were really looking forward to it. I could never forget the look on their faces. I found myself once more trying to explain the actions of their mother.

I didn't bother calling to get answers because I knew she wouldn't pick up. She would avoid me as long as she could, although our meeting was the next day. Her plans were to explain herself during the counseling session. My suspicions of her being with that guy, wouldn't allow me to wait until then. So we took a little trip over to her mom's. She wasn't there and that didn't surprise me. But man I got a big surprise. I unexpectedly discovered that she was still seeing this guy. From what I was told, she never stopped. She lied to me again; it was done to keep me at bay.

She hated when I constantly called her, over and over again. I could have cared less at that particular moment. I dialed her number until my fingers got sore. She started going off as soon as she answered the phone.

"What!" she yelled. "Stop calling me! I told you not to do that!"

"You forgot about our plans tonight?" I asked.

"No! I changed my mind about it!"

"Why? Because you're with him! I know you've still been seeing him! Still lying about it right? Guess me and your children don't matter anymore!"

"Everything that happened," she yelled, "you put it on yourself!"

We screamed at each other for a while. The fight ended when I told her to forget about getting counseled and to stay away from my house. I hung up and we went home. The children fell asleep at their grandma's, so they missed the whole bout. They slept peacefully, but I was restless for half the night. I couldn't even bring myself to lie in my own bed. It didn't feel right anymore. The sofa became my new bed and a refuge from a multitude of hurtful thoughts. It seemed easier to keep my mind off all my problems there. Thoughts of my children filled my mind instead. That kept me at peace, but still I was restless. Finally, I dosed off only to find myself dreaming about her. To me it was a dream; it would have been a nightmare for her. I knew it was GOD telling me to warn her about something.

The dream began with me receiving a call from her. It was late at night and she wanted me to come pick her up. The children and I drove to a dark wooded area we've never been before. She was inside of a store which was sitting right in the middle of the forest. There were cars and a few people standing outside. The store was crowded on the inside when I peeped in looking for her. I could hear a woman cursing up a storm. I recognized the voice, it was my wife. I made my way through the crowd and discovered she was cursing at her boyfriend; that same guy. Everybody was gathered around and watching. She looked terrible and he was quite a wreck himself. Her garments resembled that of a homeless crack head. It appeared she hadn't taken a bath nor brushed her teeth in weeks. Her hair looked like untrimmed hedges. What bothered me the most was, she didn't seem to care how she looked or carried herself. She was known for being high maintenance and for having respect for herself. I grabbed her arm and started walking toward the door. He yelled at her and held up two or three one dollar bills. He thought the money would make her come back. She cursed at him more as I pulled her outside. We were almost at the car when he came out. He yelled and held the money up again. She continued to curse at him. We got into the car and she turned toward the children.

She smiled at them and asked, "How are my babies doing?"

All they did was cry and wanted her out of the car. They were terrified of her. She started crying also, that's when I woke up. I automatically knew what the dream meant. Just didn't care about telling her at the time.

Morning came and my conscience needed serious clearing. The children were already up, still feeling the pain from the day before. I told them we were going to spend the day at one of their favorite parks.

They were more than willing to go. We packed snacks and drinks and headed out.

There wasn't going to be any counseling that day, my mind was already made up. I wasn't going. I made sure nobody knew where we were. No cell phones, pagers, or any other form of communication came with us.

They ran straight for the playground when we arrived. The

day was warm and sunny with a cool breeze blowing ever so often. I took a seat on a bench that was positioned right beside a large, freshwater pond. It was filled with wild ducks and geese, and you could see fish jumping every thirty seconds or so. There's something about water, especially a large body of it, which brings calmness to the soul. I felt as if I was in another world without problems or worries. Even the thought of all the negativity didn't bring me down. I was in complete relaxation with no one there to interrupt it. No one except my daughter, who wanted me to push her in the swing every once in a while. I didn't mind, I was still at peace. I wanted it to last forever but knew it would end soon as we got home. We were at the park from morning until late that afternoon. They all became weary and sat around me on the bench. They were ready to head home so we did.

We got home about three hours before our session was to begin. My answering machine was overflowing with messages from my wife. Most of them were her telling me to call and let her know where we were. Others were of her screaming into the phone, claiming I was wrong for not answering her calls. How ironic! She was fire hot mad. I reluctantly called her back.

"Where were you?" she asked. "We've been looking for you all day! What's the matter with you?"

"Nothing's wrong with me!" I answered. "What's wrong with you?"

"I know you're mad at me, I would be too. I know saying I'm sorry isn't gonna help either. But I know getting counseled will help."

"Counseling," I said, "I'm not going!"

"Why? You're the one who suggested it. Don't you want me back home?"

For some reason, I felt relief when she asked me that. Even after finding out she was still seeing that guy. Of course I wanted her to come home, I still loved her. I continued pretending I didn't care.

"I don't care if you come back or not!" I told her.

"I'm coming over to talk to you face to face," she said.

She was in a good mood when she got there about twenty minutes later. I allowed her to plead and beg me to go to the meeting. I told her I'd go, but only after ten minutes of her trying to convince me. She went back to her mom's as I readied myself. The plan was to drop the children there and drive to counseling in my car. That's what we did, but something happened during the time I got ready and drove to her.

Her mood changed all of a sudden. Didn't know why at first, later I realized she was preparing herself to argue at the counseling session. It was one of the longest ten minute rides of my life. There was complete silence, not a word was murmured. She stared right into the side of my head. I could see from the corner of my eye that she had the meanest looking frown on her face. I thought she was gonna take off a shoe and beat me with it, seriously. I didn't look at nor say anything to her. It felt like she wanted to kill me. She kept her eyes on me and didn't say anything the whole trip. I kept quiet and watched the road until we got there.

We arrived at the church with no words spoken at all. Our pastor greeted us as we walked into his office. He prayed and we began. He first wanted us to talk about the beginning of our relationship and when we decided to get married. Next, he wanted us to discuss problems we were having at that time. She spoke first and sounded extremely anger. She didn't discuss the present; she went way back into the past. I couldn't believe it. Almost everything she felt I did wrong to her was brought up. I retaliated with a bunch of stuff she did to me. It turned into a big argument right there in his office. It took him a while to get us under control.

"One of you involved with someone else?" he asked.

I looked right at her and didn't blink. She paused for a few seconds, and finally said, "Yes."

"You grew up in this church," he said, "You do know that this is wrong, right?"

"Yes sir, I know. But my husband has done so much to make

me so unhappy! He even kicked me out!"

"What?" I yelled. "I didn't kick you out, you left on your own!"

"Stop lying!" she yelled. "Yes you did kick me out! Did you, or did you not call my mom and tell her I needed to come live with her?"

I felt like a jackass. I allowed her to lure me into one of her traps. She knew I would never kick her out of the house. She set it up to make it seem that way. Announcing over the church that, "I hope he don't kick me out", and having me to call her mom on that one day. My pastor was present on the Sunday when she made the statement about kicking her out; he may have believed I actually did it. Also, her mom could confirm I made that phone call.

"Let's calm down," he said. He looked at her, "Tell me about this fellow."

She talked about how they met and everything in between. How he makes her feel and how he talks to her. She also mentioned the things he possessed.

"It's very exciting right? It feels like you're on cloud nine right?" my pastor asked. "Trust me, its temporary. GOD is showing me that he's done this to other women. He means you no good. You need to get out of this as soon as you can. Is he married?"

"No," she answered, "he's never been."

"I find that hard to believe," said my pastor. "I believe he's either been before or still is. Leave him alone."

Those things were not what my wife wanted to hear. She became angrier and even burst into tears. She said he tells her how much he's fallen in love with her, and he really is a good man. She tried her best to convince my pastor that she had justification for doing this. He kept telling her to get out of it.

"Well, at least she told you about em," he said to me, "most people don't say anything. When the spouse finds out, things are worse. Do you have anything to say about this?" he asked me.

"I didn't wanna mention it at first, but I feel GOD wants me to warn her."

I told them about the dream I had. He said it meant this guy was going to bring her down to a very low state. It may be physically or mentally. Whichever, it will definitely affect her self esteem. She thought it was all nonsense, didn't believe any of it. Her tears turned into a continual smirk. She said I was just trying to scare her into coming home. He said she should take heed to all of it.

We were in counseling for about two more hours. He went over Bible scriptures concerning marriage, and things such as the importance of communication in a relationship. I was taking it all in willingly; she seemed to be along just for the ride.

"So you need to cut this guy loose," he told her. "I can tell your husband is a good man and loves you very much. It's hard to find them these days. Keep this in mind. He's still young and other women are looking at him. If you leave him for this guy, and he marries someone else, you will regret it. You understand what I'm telling you?"

She gave a fake sounding, "yes sir."

"As for you young man," he said to me, "do you love your wife?"

"Yes sir I do. Very much."

"Do you want her back home again?"

"Yes sir," I answered.

"Well, there are things you must do also. Remember, she's the weakest vessel in this union. Stop getting angry and upset at her for the mistakes she's made. You wanna win her back not push her away. You gotta start doing things to win her back. Keep your communication strong and do things for her every day, watch her come running back to you. And young lady, you gotta learn to treat him like a man. You'll see a big change in him once you treat him right."

He gave us some more pointers before ending our meeting. He prayed for us. When he finished, he told us to give each other a hug. I reached out my arms, but only received a handshake from her.

"Come on, you can do better than that!" he said with a smile on his face.

She hugged and kissed me. I was very pleased with the session and thought it helped a lot. She seemed happy and revived also as we left. We got into the car and were on our way, back to my house I hoped. It didn't work out that way sorry to say. She burst into tears and started shouting at me.

"Why did you lie about having a dream? You know you where lying!"

"No I didn't!" I said. "This dream was real! Why are you so upset? I thought this meeting helped you like it did me!"

"Well it didn't! He didn't tell me nothing I wanted to hear! He only made things worse! I thought he would understand why I wanna leave you and be with this man! All these things you did to me over the years!"

We were pulling into her mother's driveway by the time she said that. We sat in the car and continued to argue.

"What about what you did to me? You ain't no angel you know! And why would you go in there bringing up stuff that happened over ten years ago?"

"Because he needed to know!" she answered.

"Why? So you could be justified for your wrong doing?"

"Yes! And I'm gonna keep on doing it! No matter what anybody says!"

She got out and walked toward the door. I called to her hoping she would come back. She ignored me.

My mind was going around in circles again as I tried to take in what had just happened. I think I went into some type of shock. I recall a massive headache and a tingling sensation in my spine. The pain increased as I watched my children come out all at once. Each of them had tears in their eyes. She must have yelled at or said something awful to them. I attempted to comfort them, but needed comforting myself.

We didn't bother getting ready for bed when we got home. They slept right there beside me on the sofa fully clothed with their shoes on. You can't even begin to imagine how awful I was feeling. I felt the counseling session was for nothing. She was right, it made things worse. I didn't know what I was going to do. All I did was sat there and stare at the wall all night. I don't remember going to sleep.

Some days went by as I struggled to rest. The only sleep I got is when I dosed off for minutes at a time, off and on. I didn't try calling her, thinking that I might upset her more. I was praying that she would contact me, and she did. She came over to get some more of her things.

"You look very tired," she said, "don't let my foolishness make you lose sleep." She kissed me and left.

That kiss gave me an ounce of hope that all was not yet lost. I prayed for her constantly. After a while, I was determined I was gonna win her back. Even when she went back to staying away weeks at a time. I wasn't going to let anything keep me from being with my wife.

I was still unemployed and still looking for work. No one was responding so I did odd jobs to help hold us over. She did something I hadn't seen her do in a long time. When she came over, she showed concern about the children having food to eat. She would leave and come right back with enough food to fill up the fridge and the pantry. She did it every time she came by. That increased my hope of us being together again.

I took the advice of my pastor and started trying to win her back. I bought her things and presented them to her when she came over. She'd thank me and leave once she found what she was looking for. Most of her belongings were still there. She got them when they were needed. I bought her cards and wrote her letters. She didn't seem to care too much for that; only cared for the pricier gifts I bought her.

Still I didn't stop; I was a determined man. When in that state, it's hard to make me quit. I started calling her and asking if she would go out with me. She said she would meet with me, but didn't show up the first three or four times. I kept my composure and kept on trying. I finally got her to go out with me.

She allowed me to pick her up one night. She introduced me to a new restaurant. I guess he took her there before. The setting and the food was fantastic. The date, on the other hand, was a whole other story.

It was terrible. I was trying to have a good time and could see she wanted the opposite. She was determined to have a terrible time. Her attitude was filthy and she snapped at me for almost anything I did. Worst of all, her mind was somewhere else. I knew it had to do with him. Still I remained calm and didn't get upset.

It was the worst date I had ever been on. I felt I wasted my money. But that was beside the point; I was only trying to get her back. I cared about her, not the date. I realized I made no progress when it was over however. When we got to her mom's, she immediately jumped out of the car without saying goodbye. I got the children and left.

The failed date caused much frustration, which caused me to scramble to come up with something else. I tried calling in an attempt to have a civil conversation with her. That was stupid of me, knowing how much she hated being called multiple times during the day. She was already upset when she answered. The whole argument was about me calling her. She told me to give up trying to win her back. She said I couldn't make her come back; she would do it when she was ready and sincerely wanted to.

To make matters worse, everybody started believing I kicked her out. She told family and friends. That was the new argument when she came over. She made herself believe I did it, knowing it never actually happened. She used it for justification. So called friends assisted her with that.

Her time away from us got longer and longer. Worrying took hold of my mind once more and this time, it affected my appetite. I would eat little if anything at all. I dropped nearly ten pounds a week for three straight weeks. I had to catch myself when people started noticing my clothes were getting too big.

My appetite gradually came back as I continued working

the odd jobs. I'd been looking for a real job for months. I don't believe I could have paid someone to hire me during that time! They were just not calling me. Thankfully, she kept bringing food over.

"Do you need anything else?" she would ask. She had to have some care for us or she wouldn't have been doing this.

I thanked her for all she did for us. I remember her coming over again, and I requested something that time.

"You ok, or do you need me to get something else?" she asked.

"No," I answered, "but I want you to do something for me."

"And what's that?" she asked.

"Please don't sleep with this guy."

With a straight face, she looked at me and said, "Ok." She turned and walked out the front door.

CHAPTER 6

Betrayal

I WAS AWAKENED one morning by someone rummaging through plastic bags and paper. I had just gone through a rough night with hardly any sleep at all. My eyes opened to witness a strange woman standing near my bed.

"Who are you and what are you doing in my house?" I asked at the top of my voice.

"Technically, it's still my house too! I'm just not here as much," she answered.

It was my wife. I would not have recognized her if she hadn't spoken. She looked as if she had been on one of those makeover shows. Nothing about her was what it had been maybe three weeks earlier. Everything was different; her hair, her clothing, her eyes and nails. Maybe I was crazy or half blind at the time, but even the shape of her body looked different. She was in our house trying on some new clothes. Clothing I never would have imagined seeing on her in my lifetime. Her skirts and pants became skin tight all of a sudden. Her blouses were tight and low cut. All of this would have been perfect for a wife trying to help spice up her marriage. Not to be worn outside of the home though.

Each time a new outfit was bought; she'd come over, try it on, and ask me how it looks. Then she'd leave and wouldn't be heard from for a week or so. Surprisingly though, she seemed more kind and polite toward me during each visit. I took it as a positive sign at first. This could be the beginning of the healing process for us. But my wife never ceased to amaze and disappoint me. The game was still on.

One particular visit, she walked in carrying a slightly smaller bag. It was one of those gift type bags, brightly colored with flower designs. You know! The ones you don't discard but keep in your closet. I was quite curious of what was in it.

"What ya got in the bag for me?" I asked kidding around. I was in one of my rare good moods during that awful time in my life.

"These are mine silly!" she said cheerfully. She emptied the contents of the bag onto the bed. "You like em?" she asked.

"Oh yeah!" I answered with excitement.

They were the sexiest underwear I had ever seen. About five or six bra and panty sets. I also understood they were the most expensive I've ever laid eyes on. Had no idea where she got them. She'd been treating me so wonderfully and we'd been getting along so well lately, that I just knew they were all for me. She put on a set and asked how they looked. They nearly drove me crazy. The room got steamy all of a sudden. But in the midst of all that excitement, there was something that needed to be made clear.

"Are these for him?" I asked with all seriousness.

"What?" she responded. "Why are you spoiling this moment? I haven't seen him in weeks. He doesn't bother me anymore. Besides, these could be for your eyes and hands only."

She walked over, kneeled down, and kissed me. The air around us began to boil.

"Yes!" I thought. "My life is finally coming back together."

She got dressed and headed for a business meeting that she and her mom had to attend. She told me to wait up for her because she would definitely be back that night. I was more than ready for my wife to come back home. But like I said, she never ceased to amaze and disappoint me. I was up until early the next day. Hadn't heard from nor had any success contacting her. Nobody, including her mom, had even seen her the night before. That so called business meeting was nothing short of a fluke.

She showed up again about a week later. We rumbled once more by shouting at each other. I expressed how I was growing very tired of those senseless games. I was getting fed up of her constantly making a fool of me. No longer did I wanna give her the benefit of the doubt. She kept denying that she was still seeing him, but any idiot could tell she was lying. It was so obviously written across her face. We fought about it constantly. She would storm out of the house in anger, return days later, and storm out again after another fight. Though I held onto a pixel of hope, reality kept reminding me that this marriage was likely at the end of the road. I'll never forget it, the night when that spec of hope disappeared and reality took its toll.

It happened on a stormy Saturday night. The rain was pounding the roof and the wind howled like a pack of wolves. For some reason, my mind was going in every direction known to man. I watched videos and did whatever I could to occupy it. Nothing seemed to work. What was the deal? What was going on? The answer; the fact that a good man's life was turning upside down, in such a small period of time, took hold. And it was a tight grip. I stretched out across my bed, called out to GOD, and just cried. I couldn't stop. My children made their way to my door and watched. They didn't say anything but I knew they were there. Didn't ask what was wrong with me, just stood by the door and watched. My daughter broke the silence. She was the only one that had been asleep during the bad storm. It awakened and must have frightened her too.

"Daddy! Is Mommy ok?" She asked with a trembling voice.

I held my hand out and she walked over to me. She got in the bed to lie down beside me.

"She's all right," I said as I put my arm around her.

My sons must have figured everything was ok then. They weren't there when I raised my head up to look. My daughter's presence comforted me that night. It allowed me to get some much needed rest.

My wife showed up about two weeks later. We actually

talked without arguing. She looked as if something was eating her up inside.

"What's wrong?" I asked.

"I've been a bad person the last few months," she answered, "you know that, right?"

"We've all done bad things, but GOD forgives us," I said, trying to cheer her up.

"Yeah but," she paused.

"What's wrong?" I asked again.

"It's nothing. Let's go get something to eat. I'll buy."

We drove to a nearby restaurant and ordered some carryout. We got the food and headed back toward the house. We had a peaceful conversation, but something was still bothering her. I was afraid to ask what it was. That really didn't matter. She let me in on it regardless. Of all the news a man could receive from his spouse, in my opinion, this is probably the worst. It is the ultimate spousal betrayal. I don't understand why she decided to tell me at that time. Maybe the guilt overwhelmed her.

"I gotta tell you this. I can't keep it in no longer," she said.

I kept silent and listened. She got straight to the point.

"I've been sleeping with this guy."

I don't think I need to explain what I was feeling at that moment. But I had to make sure I heard her correctly.

"What?" I asked.

"I've been sleeping with him," she said.

My blood and I'm guessing every other fluid in my body was boiling after that statement.

"How could you do this to me?" I yelled as I pounded the dashboard. "You said you wouldn't do that! You said you'll never go that far! Why did you destroy our marriage like this?"

Tears were flowing down her face by then. "I'm sorry! I didn't expect anything like this to ever happen to us either! I don't know what came over me! It first happened the night we had counseling! I don't know, I guess I was so angry with you and our pastor that I didn't care anymore!"

"You gotta be kidding me!" I yelled. "You acted like a whore on the night we got marriage counseling! Are you nuts?"

"I'm sorry!" she said as she covered her face and cried even harder.

"Yeah, you should be!" I yelled. "Don't you say another word to me! When we get home, get whatever you got there and get out!"

I was mad enough to kill somebody. She cried all the way home and I didn't say anything else until we got through the front door.

"How could you do this to me?" I yelled as I broke down in tears. I couldn't remember crying like that since I was a baby. I got on my knees and she wrapped her arms around my neck. I wrapped my arms around her. We both stayed there and cried for a while.

"I'm so sorry," she kept saying.

I got angrier and pushed her away from me. "Don't you touch me!" I yelled and stood up. She tried to hug me again. "I said don't touch me!" I went into my bedroom and stared at that picture we took together. You know; the one with the poem I wrote her in the background. I grabbed it and walked back into the living room.

"You see this!" I yelled as I held it up.

"Please don't do this," she said. "No!" she yelled as I dropped it.

Then I smashed it with my foot, breaking out all the glass.

"This is what our marriage meant to you!" I yelled. "Now this is what you mean to me!"

She came over and pulled the picture and the poem from the wrecked frame. I stepped into the bedroom to keep from looking at her. My head was pounding so I covered both my temples with my hands.

She came in and spoke with my back turned to her. "I don't know what else to say other than I'm sorry," she said softly.

"There's nothing else you can say," I said, "it'll be best if you leave right now."

"I'm so sorry," she said then left my house.

Now, I might be wrong, and some will argue this issue. This is just my opinion. I truly believe this is tougher on a man than on a woman. Yeah, the cheating spouse! I've heard that women are easier to forgive a cheating spouse than men are. I don't know how true any of this is, but I do know I was ready to kill somebody. Not only did I feel a sacred covenant was broken between us, but my pride and confidence were shattered to pieces. I thought about doing something crazy in the public. Like catching them together and just gunning them down. Or maybe kidnapping them and forcing her to watch as I beat him to death. I knew it was the devil messing with my mind. Satan even tried to use my family to convince me to do something stupid.

A relative of mine was in law enforcement and said he could make it happen. I would get away with it clean handedly. I wasn't that crazy. This was premeditated murder. Besides, I still loved her.

I would spend the next few days doing nothing but sitting around. I didn't eat nor drink for a day or two. I just sat around in a distant stare doing nothing. The only people I had contact with were my children. It even took time for me to respond to anything they said! I wouldn't answer the phone nor go anywhere. I was sinking into depression like never before. Only the thought of my children kept me afloat. I knew I had to pull myself up if I was to continue taking care of them. If I was gone, no one else would see to them like I was seeing to them. Regardless of all the difficulties, some strength had to remain. I gradually began doing things around the house again. It's always a good idea to keep busy, I learned, when such turmoil befalls you. I eventually started going back outside again. I did my best to avoid people as much as possible. I was hoping not to answer any questions concerning my wife. Didn't wanna lie about her to anybody! I managed well.

The title, "Single Dad", is one I felt it was time to start preparing for. The thoughts of what my wife did needed to be put aside to make room for that preparation. Easier said than done, huh? She overshadowed anything that had ever gone through my mind. My brain was just flooded with unbelief and grief and needed serious draining. It had to be done in order for us to move forward. I did whatever I could to forget about her. Nothing seemed to work. All the dirt she did crushed me, but a part of me still wanted to be with her. Couldn't understand what was happening to me.

I've heard many stories of other men involved in similar situations. Some of them actually cheated on their wives first. When their wives cheated, all of them said they were done and wouldn't have anything else to do with her. So what was my problem? I still wanted her to come home. I thought about calling her too. Apparently she was thinking about calling me; that's just what she did.

She apologized every other sentence or two during our conversation. It was going good until she said, "I wish I could cut myself in half and be with both of you."

Of course that ticked me off. I just hung up without a warning. I was her husband; she should have been willing to give herself to me one hundred percent. Not fifty percent to some other man. She called back and apologized for saying it. But she said it at least three more times. I hung up each time.

Our phone sessions got better once she stopped saying it. The phone was our only contact with each other for weeks to come. As I tried to convince her to come home, she tried to make me believe things will never work the same for us again. Her actions were too extreme she felt. My true belief is, she thought I would get her home just to get back at her. You know, go out and cheat then come home and inform her about it. Throw it in her face right before I threw her outta my house. She knew I wasn't that type of person although she was feeling that way. What else was there to do? We continued to call each other.

One would probably think that all this mess would cause a person to have some form of a mental breakdown. Fortunately, I was taking the whole ordeal pretty well. Talking with my wife everyday helped out a lot. But there comes a time in everyone's life when that wrong chord is finally struck. I mean the big one. The one that makes you completely go off. It happened to me on the day my wife decided to make an unannounced visit.

She came through the front door and immediately wrapped her arms around my neck. "I miss you so much," she said as I wrapped my arms around her waist.

She told me she was tired and ready to come home. She and her boyfriend hadn't been getting along lately. There's been a lot of arguing, matter of fact; they'd just had a major one. She was ready to cut him loose and looked more sincere than ever about it.

The day I was hoping for had come right out of the blue. I was the happiest man on Earth. My spouse had returned to me. What she said next shocked me. She told me to make love to her. So we did, passionately!

Later that evening, I ran a few chores and did a couple of repairs on her car. There wasn't anything I wouldn't do for her at that moment. She sent me off to the store to pick up a few things. Got what she wanted and made it back in about thirty minutes. I walked in and could hear her in the bedroom. She was talking on her cell phone and must not have heard me come in. I thought nothing of it and headed toward the room. Something she said stopped me dead in my tracks.

"What are you wearing?" she asked the person on the phone.

The way it sounded, unless she was gay, indicated it was a male on the other end. I decided to wait and listen for a minute. It was the same ole game and I got played again. Why did she want to sleep with me but be with that guy? Didn't know the answer right then, but found out why a couple of months later. I overheard her talking to someone about him. I'll be as discreet as I can with this answer. Let's just say, he had problems satisfying her.

So I continued to listen. Guess they made up since having the fight earlier; during the time I was at the store for her. There were some things said about me but that didn't set me off. What did it is when he was trying to hang up but she wouldn't let him.

"I don't wanna hang up right now," she said with the voice of a little girl. "I want you to keep talking to me!"

I burst into the room and went ballistic. She hung up the phone without saying goodbye. She became angrier than I was. Guess she didn't expect to get caught so red handedly! We yelled from one room to the next. We argued about nearly everything we had done wrong to each other. Even the garage was not immune to our shouting. The garage door was up so I slammed it down as hard as I could. So hard that it set off the burglar alarm that wasn't even armed at the time. I had to disconnect the power to shut it off. It still alerted the police because they were on our block shining their spotlight at every house. The lack of power prevented them from locating the correct address. And that was a good thing. They probably would have found a reason to arrest me, with all the shouting going on.

This, without a doubt, was the worst verbal rumble I had ever had in my life. We scrapped until early the next morning. She cursed at me and I pounded the walls. That was an awful event. We took about a fifteen minute break to get the children back in bed after waking them. Then we started up again. Her phone rang and it was him. I allowed her to answer it only because there was something I wanted to do. She stepped into another room as I sneaked up behind her.

"I'm sorry for hanging up on you last night," she said, "can I call you back later?"

I snatched the cell phone as she waited for an answer. This is when I went off on him. She tried to get it back, but I kept her hands away. I threatened him, told him what would happen if I saw him again. After a minute of threats, she was able to retrieve the phone while my back was turned. Didn't say anything else to him, just hung it up. Then all was quiet. We stood there silently and she was totally embarrassed. She spoke up after a while.

"I'm leaving!" she said.

"Good! And you don't have to come back!" I replied.

"Maybe I won't!" she said. "By the way," she looked me straight in the face, "I never loved you! I was only here for the money!"

"Guess you never loved your children either!" I said.

"Well, I didn't wanna have em!" Then she left.

Whether that was true or not, I don't know. But I did know this; like a helium balloon that was punctured with a sharp pin, my feelings for her started seeping out. I could feel it right then and there. Hatred began setting in.

All day I thought about what she said. I wanted very much to get back at both of them. I attempted to call and threaten him some more. That would've also gotten her pretty upset. I called a number that I thought was his. I left a very harsh and gruesome message; to the wrong person believe it or not! Two or three hours later, someone from that number called me back. It belonged to a very nice lady.

"Why did you leave this message on my machine?" she asked.

I apologized and explained what happened. I gave her a few details of my troubles. She understood completely. She said she would have done a lot more than leave messages. She would have gotten a weapon and went looking for them.

"They ain't even worth it," I said. "Besides, I got children to raise."

"Yeah, you're right," she replied. "Just wait and see, they'll get what's coming to em. They always do."

I apologized again for calling her phone and leaving that message. I was relieved she was such a nice person. Still I would have hated to be in the shoes of someone that she was pursuing with a weapon in her hand. Because she seemed nice didn't necessarily mean she didn't know how to be ruthless. I actually enjoyed talking to her about my problems a while longer before we hung up. Now back to my wife!

Later, I discovered my wife was taking out of town trips to see this fellow. Her store sales had begun dwindling and she was becoming a very unwise business person. She'd use the little money she did make to buy plane tickets to visit him. The store didn't seem to matter anymore. I didn't care; she didn't matter to me anymore!

I only cared about me and my children. Nothing was gonna stop me from being the world's greatest dad. Nothing or nobody! Not even a disastrous marriage or a cheating spouse. But I would be put to the test as more tough times headed our way.

CHAPTER 7

A Time To Let Go

MANY BAD THINGS happen to us as we live this life. It doesn't matter how good or bad of a person we are, bad times will come. I believe the reason for most of it is, to help us grow and become stronger. GOD has a purpose for each of our lives. We go through hardships and gain strength as we climb each mountain that sits in our path. We are stronger, therefore able to serve our purpose more effectively.

Of course my strengthening started with that guy interrupting my marriage. Well, it weakened me before it made me stronger. Boy was I weak! Both mentally and physically! Most of the mental damage was pretty much done within the first few weeks. My body wasn't hit hard until after that last big argument. I could feel the sickness coming over me. A bunch of stress and drama could actually cause pain in your body. Worrying caused me to have constant headaches. Taking aspirin or pain killers didn't help soothe the pain at all. Though I never checked it, I knew my blood pressure was sky high. My pulse felt like it wanted to thump right out of my veins. Also, my appetite was way past pathetic; wasn't eating much at all. When I did begin forcing myself to, I would eat one meal every other day or two. I remember dropping a lot of weight again; a lot of pounds in a two week period. A lack of nutrition and high metabolism contributed to that.

My mental and physical breakdowns were some of the first mountains I needed to cross. My hatred for her proved to be my

Mount Everest.

The more I thought about her, the more I hated her. Believe me when I say I thought about her constantly. The hurt she put on me was a pain I never felt before. I've had breakups in the past. Even had an ex-girlfriend who played games similar to the ones my wife played. I bought things for her, but she gave them to the guy whom she was truly interested in. I let her borrow an expensive jacket too. She had no plans to return it because it was a gift for him. Her scheme was uncovered when I met another fellow she was doing the same things to. We surprised her at her boyfriend's house and got our things back. What this girl did didn't hurt me one bit, unlike the breakup with my wife. Those past relationships were child's play and not serious at all. My marriage was serious business.

My wife must have sensed my feelings because she stayed away at the time. That was probably a good idea. I might have done something that I might still be regretting until this day. Half of my thoughts concerned ways I could get back at her. Taking my children away and never seeing her again crossed my mind. I would instill hatred for her in them as they grew up. That guaranteed them disrespecting her, in case they ever saw her again. I thought about spreading her business all over our church; only a few people knew about it at the time. The embarrassment would have been so great, she'd probably not return there anymore. Also, my hatred triggered thoughts of sleeping with her so called female friends that would have allowed me to. There was quite a few that wouldn't have mind. That's what I was told. I would have filmed it and shown it to her. My wife would have blown a fuse and maybe even tried to kill me. There were many more things I thought about doing, but I dare not say.

My hatred was deepened as I thought about her lack of concern when she departed from her young children. I compared her to my dad when he left. I remember him living with us when we were very young. He moved out, but we would still see him a lot. He even kept us on the weekends. Then he just disappeared. We eventually saw him again, once every three to five years. That was painful. What if my wife was absent for years at a time? Would my children feel the frustration I felt? Would they suffer emotionally like I did?

At one point in my teenage years, I thought it was unusual for a dad to play sports with his child. I heard my friend say he played basketball with his dad. I remember asking him about it. My friends thought I was nuts when I said, "you play ball with ya dad!" A dad playing sports with his child was something I'd never heard of or just never paid attention to. My dad did nothing like that with me. At first, it didn't bother me. But when it sunk in, I was so angry at him. I hated him for a long time. I missed out on experiences other children had because he wasn't there for me.

The devil tried to use every negative moment in my past, which related to something my wife was doing, to cause me to hate her more. Satan was trying to take control of me. If things kept heading downward, he would have and I would've died. He was just doing his job and he's good at it. That's if we allow him to be. I helped him out for a while by not praying to the LORD. In the midst of all the evil going on around me, I neglected to. But GOD still loves us so much, even when we do wrong. He loves us like we love our children and would do anything for us. He proves it whenever we go through a catastrophe like this. He's the small still voice that gives us the advice we need to hear at the right moment.

His advice to me was, "JUST LET GO!"

I had to let her go and everything else that was hindering me. I had to extinguish all that hatred that got embedded in my heart. Not only for her, for the hatred toward all other women too. I'd convinced myself to never trust them again. Nevertheless, I was gonna sleep with as many as possible.

Those ill feelings had to be removed in order for me to move forward. That wasn't easy to do, but it didn't take as long as you would have thought. So what should I have done? Anything I could to get my mind off all my misfortune.

Movies became a huge part of me and my children's lives.

The video stores made a killing from all the DVDs we bought and rented. We watched them constantly whenever we were at home. Most of them were comedy or anything that would keep us laughing. We all know laughter is a cure for all sorts of problems. It sure helped me a whole lot. I avoided films that were similar or related to what I was going through. I needed nothing to remind me of it.

We visited the zoo more frequently. I've always loved animals and being at the zoo. My children must have inherited it from me. Like me, they wanted to stay all day and see all the animals at least twice. The zoo was good exercise for both the body and mind.

The thing we did most was visit the city parks; at least four days a week, and a different one each day. Some had hiking trails where we could just walk and talk for hours. Others had large ponds or lakes which were filled with all types of wildlife. We all had a good time.

Of course we played sports, mostly football and Frisbee. Of course my daughter preferred being at the playground. I got a lot of workouts pushing her on the swings and merry-go-round. There was one particular park that proved to be the most relaxing. In its huge wide open field, we would just lie out in the grass and watch the sky. It would be covered with kites and clouds of all shapes. Just like being in a wonderful dream! You could just dream all your problems away. Felt I was close to doing just that.

Somebody once told me that it took five years for an individual to heal from the death of a loved one. That might be an actual fact; I never counted the years when it happened to me. I tried to go on with life as soon as possible. Now what about the healing process time for broken marriages? For a husband with a cheating spouse. I don't think I've ever heard the numbers on that one. So I don't know. What I do know is there has to be forgiveness. The Bible says we must forgive no matter what was done to us. How do I know I forgave my wife? Well, when I thought of what she did, it didn't upset me anymore. I'd gotten to the point where there was neither bitterness nor hatred for her. I laughed when I thought about it from then on.

Completely forgiving a cheating spouse does not mean you have to remarry her/him. Some folks believe you must and will debate you about it. But you don't have to. If you could get along and not be angry with them because of what they've done, then they've been forgiven. Just wanted to put that out there!

It became a positive, a life learning experience. My marriage taught me many do's and don'ts concerning relationships. Even talked to my wife and us both laughed about the whole thing. Oh yeah, you must find common ground also. We had to get along rather we were together or not. For GOD's sake, we got children together! It is important that children see their parents cooperating at all times. Bickering or trying to get revenge on one another, could definitely affect the young mind in a major way. And it will be a disastrous way.

Like stated above, I don't know the numbers on this one. Heard many tales in which it took years for some folks to heal. Many never recovered at all. What their ex's did affected their future relationships. They took their pain out on other potential lifetime mates. If anything went wrong, it was related to something that horrible ex did in the past. I wouldn't dare think of being with someone if I was carrying all that dirty baggage. Maybe that's why I was so fortunate in this. I got over what my wife did in a matter of months. Only a few months at that! I still had to be healed in other areas, but I was cured of my breakup.

We continued to talk, my wife and I. We spoke as if we'd never been married or in any intimate relationship. Just like best buddies, we discussed past and current events. My main topic was our children, as you may have figured. Hers was mainly about her boyfriend. How wonderful and adventurous he was. They even discussed getting married. He was already calling her his wife. That's what he called her when he left messages on her answering service. That didn't bother me at all. Matter of fact, the thought of him marrying her seemed to have lifted a heavy burden off me. That was a strange feeling.

CHAPTER 8

A Peaceful Divorce

"SHHHH, BE QUIET; he's on the phone," my wife whispered to me. She'd been doing that lately when we hung out. Her man began having issues with her being around me. She never did admit that for some reason. She'd tell me to be quiet then say all is well. I knew what was going on, but didn't care. Why would I? Every last one of my feelings for her had vanished. Here's some proof. In the past when guys stared at or flirted with her, I'd get mad. Even had a word or two for some of them. But right then, I could have cared less.

I wanted to tell them, "She's not with me anymore!"

Whatever happened after that would be between the flirting guy and her boyfriend. All I would do is sit back and enjoy the show, if I was there. She told me he was much worse than I was concerning this. He would go off if a guy looked at her for a millisecond. I thought it was crazy and that she needed to watch herself.

I found myself being around her more than I wanted to be. She wanted to hang out and gossip about all the drama that was happening in her life. Not only with him, but with her friends and the people around the store also. There were more and more men hitting on her when they discovered we were apart. I'm guessing they thought they had a chance since she left her husband for somebody else.

She loved all that attention from those guys. There was one fellow, a charlatan, who claimed to be from out of town. He had a ring that needed to be sized for his girlfriend. Not knowing where to have it done, he asked my wife to do it for him. He gave her the money to have it done plus a little extra for her pockets. When it was finished he came to pick it up. She handed it to him, but he told her she could keep it. Apparently, he and his girlfriend broke up. He wanted my wife to keep the ring but she didn't. Still, the knucklehead asked her to go out with him. It was all a trick. He thought she would be impressed by the money he blew off on the ring. He kept coming around and eventually had an exchange with her boyfriend. That intimidated him. It put an end to whatever he was trying to accomplish.

I felt a little sorry for her boyfriend. He had his hands full with her craving for all that attention; what a horrible feeling! But he was the one she wanted in spite of the attention. Like stated earlier, most of the chatter was about him. She was beginning to fall deeply in love with him and saw herself with nobody else. She would neglect to open the store in order to spend the day with him. She called him constantly when he wasn't in town. She got to where she couldn't sleep without having him on the phone. He was her sleeping pill; she'd fall asleep with the phone up against her ear every night.

She was completely comfortable talking to me about him. I don't think she cared if it bothered me or not. I would have been completely on edge talking to her about my girlfriend. Hers was a peculiar situation. It's not often that you see spouses or soon to be ex's having a friendly talk about their new mates. Especially not that early in a separation. She's a very odd person and that was nothing strange to her.

We continued doing things with the children. We even got her to go to the zoo and stay longer than thirty minutes. Once, she stayed a whopping two hours. I think it was only because he called her. She talked on the phone and forgot where she was. Of course we had to be quiet while she chatted with him. I hated that with a passion, but I did it anyway. It was something I didn't want to argue about. Seeing my children enjoying themselves was more important. I got so use to her quieting us when he called, that it stopped bothering me. She even did it while we were in the supermarket. I became proactive; started moving away from her before she had a chance to quiet me down. It felt better that way.

I was actually kind of proud of her. Her being at the zoo longer than thirty minutes hadn't occurred in a long time. She was thinking more of her children than of herself for a change. Nevertheless, some good things happen only to come to an end.

The subject of divorce rose again as our main topic of discussion. It was there to stay until we ultimately did it. He told her he wanted to get married. That made her extremely adamant to getting a divorce. I was the only one standing in the way. I truly wanted it too, but played with her for a while. Being the victim in the whole ordeal gave me the right to have a little fun. Man it was fun too! I'll never forget how much she begged me. She never begged that much for anything before. She'd call late at night and wake me out of my sleep about it. That was fun although she disturbed me from my rest. When the game got boring, I went ahead and agreed to the divorce. I decided to let them have each other.

So we went and filed for it together. We joked and laughed all the way there and were in an excellent mood upon arrival. The folks at the lawyer's office tried their best to talk us out of it. They thought we were the world's happiest couple and that our problems could be worked out.

"You two look like you belong together," this one guy said.

"Looks are deceiving," I replied.

"Really," he said, "You seem to get along so well. Most couples we deal with can't be in the same room together. Tell me why you guys want a divorce."

We talked about everything that happened since our break-up at the start of the year. We discussed problems in the past and at that present time. My wife explained how she was in love and wanted to marry this new guy. I told him I had no problems with that; my feelings for her were gone anyway. I couldn't picture myself loving her like I use to. I think he got the idea.

"Wow, that's rough!" he said. "Exactly how long have you two been married?"

"Ten years," we both answered.

"I've been dating my girlfriend for five years," he said, "I was thinking about asking her to marry me. I think I'm gonna think about it some more now that I've talked to you two. You got me scared to death!"

Hearing that made me think about something. Sometimes we don't know whose looking up to us or how others are influenced by us until something major takes place. You'll be stunned by who's watching. Since our split, people were approaching from all directions.

They said things like, "I never thought I would see you two apart in my lifetime." Also, "This makes me not wanna get married."

What shocked me the most was all the couples that fell apart after our marriage collapsed. It was like we made the decision for them. It looked as if they watched and waited to see what we were going to do. They were already on the rocks; guess they needed some extra motivation. I felt guilty at first, but everyone has to choose their own paths.

So we finished filing. I had no idea that a divorce was so complicated. There were so many regulations and steps that had to be taken in order for it to be final. We had to decide where the children were going to live. That was easy because she left them with me anyway. In our state, we both had to get life insurance. That was because of the children of course.

We also had to attend a one day class pertaining to post divorce behavior. It was very interesting with no dreary moments at all. The instructor's main focus was geared toward the children. There are people selfish enough who'd use their offspring to deceive an ex spouse. He spoke of one lady who used her son to lie to his dad on a weekly basis. The son would say he needed money for certain things but gave it all to his mom. She was already receiving child support. It was all about revenge and disrupting her ex-husband's life.

The lesson that caught my attention the most dealt with the things we say about our ex's in the presence of others. Your words could come back and bite you. We should make it a habit to not say anything negative about our ex, or allow anyone else to while our children are present. You don't want them believing it or repeating it in front of your ex. It can cause dilemmas you've never experienced before. My soon-to-be ex especially needed to hear that lesson.

We received a certificate of completion at the conclusion of the class. It had to be presented to the judge who was given the task of finalizing the divorce. This class came a few months later after filing for our split.

We left the lawyer's office after getting our court date. It was to occur exactly six months after the date we filed. My soon to be ex suggested we should go out and celebrate. That's strange huh, celebrating a divorce! Strange it was but it didn't feel that way at the time. Crazier things had happened within that twelve month time frame. So this type of celebration was no big deal. We did it by having dinner at one of our favorite restaurants.

"So how do you feel?" she asked.

"Feels like most of the pressure left," I answered. "What about you?"

"I'm actually okay now. Especially knowing that you're okay."

"Yeah, I've been great for a while now. Things could have been a lot worse you know."

"I know that's right!" she said as we tapped our drinks together.

We joked and laughed about a bunch of stuff that occurred that year. We got the attention of one of the waiters working that night. He knew us well because he waited on us regularly.

"Hey, I haven't seen you guys in a while," he said. Thought you moved away or something."

"Yeah, we're still here my man," I said.

"Looks like you're celebrating something. What's the big event?"

"You wouldn't believe it if we told you," said my wife.

"Try me anyway!" he said.

"All right," she said, "We just filed for divorce not three hours ago."

"No friggin way! Not you two! You look perfect together! You were right; I don't believe it!"

"Well, you better start believing!" I said. "This could be the last time you see us here together."

"Man, that sure makes me wanna get married real soon!" he said with cynicism as he walked away.

Like I said earlier, we had that impact on a lot of folks. But there could have been a silver lining to it. Maybe some of them thought they were ready for marriage, but in truth were not. We may have helped them in the long run; helped them to avoid years of pain and grief.

Whether we helped or not, we were still at the restaurant celebrating. About two hours later, we were at the end of our fiesta. We paid the check and I drove her home.

"You remember that bad stuff I said to you?" she asked as we pulled into her mom's driveway.

"You gotta be just a bit more specific," I responded, "Cause you said a ton of bad things to me!"

"You're so silly!" She said as she laughed. "I mean about me never loving you and not wanting my children."

I paused briefly, "yeah I remember."

"You know I really didn't mean those things."

"For real! You could have fooled me!" I said jokingly.

She looked at me with a serious smirk.

"I'm just kidding! I know you really didn't mean it," I said as we hugged.

She kissed me on the cheek and went inside the house.

CHAPTER 9

Manifestation

"HELLO!" I ANSWERED the phone after rushing to pick it up. I was in the garage and tried to grab it before it stopped ringing. It was my soon to be ex and her boyfriend on three way. It was early in the morning and they were screaming at each other. They were arguing about what a woman's place should be in the home. These two individuals, the people behind the greatest downturn of my life, were actually seeking my opinion about something. It was unbelievable! They both wanted me to disagree with the other. I couldn't help laughing about it.

He'd say something like, "a woman needs to do her job at home and also work and make her own money!"

She'd respond, "You've lost your mind. The man is supposed to bring in all the income and help around the house too. Matter of fact, you should take complete care of me!"

That remark started them screaming again. They went on and on and on, while I was still on the line. I had no choice but to interrupt.

"You two work this out on your own!" I said then hung up the phone.

Going by what I was told, that phone call is when their arguments began. She was on her phone fighting with him every time I saw her. The things they quarreled about made little to no sense at all. They were less significant than the things she and I fought about. I mean, come on! How can anyone fight over the way a certain food tastes? I don't know the answer to that, but I know they did it. If I needed a good laugh, I'd just listen to them argue. I hope I didn't sound that ridiculous when I argued with her.

Their squabbles appeared to be getting out of control. They did it constantly, even while at work. Both in person and on the telephone. She could be heard yelling at him from her store. He'd shout back from his job. It was horrible and for some reason, she stopped letting people know what the disputes were about. I wanted to ask, but didn't wanna start one that was aimed at me. Especially the ones in which she was really letting him have it! I'm not sure, but I think I heard her use curse words I never heard before. That's how intense and wild the situation got.

Anyone could tell she was becoming very stressed out. We were too afraid to ask though. She eventually admitted it herself. Sleep was lost and she suffered migraines just about daily. Thankfully though, the big fights ended for a season. Her chances of getting sick because of high blood pressure or something was halted temporarily. But the end was not yet.

It was discovered that she was pressuring him to marry her. He kept telling her he would in good time. That wasn't good enough for her. My soon to be ex needed to be sure he was serious about her. She demanded an engagement ring.

I don't know about anyone else whose reading this, but I'll tell you how I feel about that. If a woman has to demand a ring from a fellow to show he's truly serious about marrying her, something's wrong. That's just my opinion though.

She stayed on him about it day and night. That became their next big argument. She wouldn't give him a minute to breathe; if not on the phone, then in person. Everything would be going good with them when he was in town. Then all of a sudden, she'd mention the ring. The subject brought out Mr. Hyde in their relationship. Guess she got angry when thinking about it; he got angry when pressured about it. Two heated beings make a bad combination.

He must have gotten sick of her nagging. It took probably a

month for him to finally give her one. I believed he cared very much for her and was in fact serious about getting married. He just needed more time; for reasons that were uncovered later on.

She was like a little girl flashing her new ring at folks. It gave her the best feeling in the world. She was engaged to the man of her dreams. Everybody thought she had it made.

"You left your husband and almost immediately got engaged to a better man!" they'd say. "How did you do it?"

To make things look even better, he bought a new car. It would be hers as soon as they got married. He drove it to town and let her keep it each time he was there. She flaunted it all around the city all day long.

"Check out my new car!" she told friends and family.

Everybody got a chance to ride in it, including my children. I didn't like them being in it one bit. She tried to get me to ride in it. I wanted no part of it. I thought about the time she let him ride in my car. That wasn't right and it wasn't right for me to ride in his.

"Come on, feel how it rides!" she'd say to me.

"No thanks!" I'd respond. "I'll drive my own car."

"Well, if you change your mind or need it for anything just let me know."

"Not gonna happen!" I said. "Thanks but no thanks!"

I'm led to believe I'm the only person she knew that didn't ride in it. It was loaded with different people each time I saw her drive by. She looked like a teenager driving her parent's new ride. Showing off for her teenage buddies! Just having a good time!

He did all this for a reason, the ring and the car. My theory is, the ring was to keep her quiet and the car was to seal the deal. You know, to really show how severe his feelings were for her. Also, he needed assurance that she would not leave him. She left me, remember? And we were already married. I had to give him his props, he was using his brains. She had not one single clue. The thought of what he was doing may not have entered her mind at all. Guess all the excitement clouded her thinking at the moment.

Things were then grander than ever between them. She started going out of town to visit him and stayed for a whole week sometimes. She returned with tons of gifts and tales of all the exhilarating events that took place. A host of new and interesting faces got acquainted with her. Unfortunately for him, some were his co-workers; many were his close friends. Well, they were supposed to be. A number of his buddies recognized her because they visited her store also. They never took the time to get to know her like he did. That all changed when they saw that she was dating him. And a big change it was.

A good way to learn if a friend is truly your friend is to allow them to meet the person you're dating. Their actions will determine that for you. He got his answer loud and clear.

One by one, they began hanging out at her store for hours at a time. They made sure her fiancé was not around. She believed they were good friends and meant no harm. They were just trying to make him look better and on top of that, they never made a pass at her. That was the good news. Everything else answered that question of friendship. That was the bad news.

She received some unexpected information while talking with one of them one evening. Apparently it slipped out by mistake; he thought it out loud. That's what the guy told her. I think it was entirely done on purpose. Matter of fact, I believe it was planned from the time he found out about them. Why would it even be on his mind at that very second? To cause trouble, that's why!

The info had to do with her fiancé having a fling with another woman who worked in her building. It happened a few months before he met my soon to be ex. Still it infuriated her. Not because it happened, but because of who it happened with. Let's just say the other woman had an undesirable reputation. She was the lowest form of life according to her fiancé. He was a hypocrite, often telling my wife he would never touch a woman like that. It made him look incredibly bad never saying anything positive about the woman; nevertheless, he was involved with her.

The ordeal sparked a new round of serious fights. They ended up being some of the worst ones yet. She questioned him about the fling and he kept denying it for a while. The more he denied it, the more she asked about it. I don't know what made him finally confess to it, but I know he wished he hadn't.

My wife fell straight off her rocker. From the time she first heard about it up until his confession, there was a glimmer of hope she held on to. The hope that no matter how long or how much she examined him, he would always say no. That would have given her confidence that he actually didn't do it. I call it (being in denial with peace). Too bad for the guy! He did do it and she unmercifully let him have it.

"Hello," I answered when she called me one morning.

"Hey," she responded, "I've been doing some crazy stuff lately."

"What? Not you!" I said teasingly.

"I'm serious! He left and won't answer his phone."

"What did you do?" I asked.

"Well, we've been fighting a lot since I found out about that girl down at the store. When I say I've been fighting, I mean it literally. I hit him with my fist or with whatever I could find."

"Wait a minute!" I interrupted. "You said you hit him?"

"Yeah!"

"Did he hit you?"

"No!" she yelled. "He ain't stupid! He knows I'd kill him if he did! All he does is hold me off and tries to get away."

"You hit him! Why?"

"I don't know. When I see him, I imagine him being with that girl. It makes me mad and I start fussing about it. He gets mad and tries to make her out better than me. That's when I start throwing punches and he runs and ducks!"

That's entertaining right? A man running from flying bottles, pots and pans, or whatever! Pretty funny huh! Well, there's nothing funny about it. They weren't even married yet and were already into physical conflicts. The warning signs should have been going berserk. They were, but nobody noticed them. They never do until after the fact; like me.

Things cooled down and went back to normal. Well, for maybe two weeks. Info about his life came in from all directions. His good buddies were the main culprits. It was like a competition to see who would drop the biggest dime on him. Other co-workers were encouraged to join in on the action. They couldn't wait to meet and enlighten her on what they knew about his life. Everybody wanted to join the dance. Even one of the local lesbians offered to do a background check on him; at no cost to my wife. She was nuts about my soon-to-be ex, but hated him. Heard he didn't care much for her either. They had problems clicking the first day they met; I heard.

My soon to be ex's brain was overloaded with a whole encyclopedia of information. Man, talk about a world of confusion! There were so many stories contradicting the words of her fiancé. Their main focus was on his possessions.

He hardly owned anything according to them. He lived in a small apartment and owned no houses. But what about the house he showed her when she visited one day? They said it was a house he attempted to buy when he started dating her. He wanted to cover his tracks in case she wanted to see where he lived. Guess he removed the (For Sale) sign before she got into town. She uncovered the true reason why they stayed in a hotel when she visited. It wasn't because his house was being renovated like he said.

What about those magnificent vehicles? Were they really his?

"Of course they were! Until he took them back to where he rented them from!" said his friends.

Before he met her, he drove an old beat-up lemon. He also had an old SUV that was in terrible condition. It sounded like the engine was gonna jump out. He did actually buy the new car that was to go to her after the wedding. The problem with that was, he was still paying for it and didn't pay it off with cash like he said. Also, it was older than she thought and he got a real good discount on it. They said it was something he did to help cover his tracks.

Basically, the property, the businesses, and all the other big ticket items he owned were a myth. He was just another regular ole Joe. No bigger than the next man. But she was skeptical and who could blame her? That was a lot of astounding information from strangers. And we all know what she did next; confronted him about it!

"They're all jealous!" he said. "These guys been after me since we started working together! I knew they really weren't my friends! I just went along with the game! Guess I enjoyed watching what they would do next."

Those were encouraging words to hear. She felt much better knowing they were only trying to split them up. He was very upset so she stayed with him that night. She was there to comfort and keep him relaxed. Even gave him a back massage. Afterward, he took a shower. She noticed he forgot to take his wallet. He normally kept it with him at all times because he didn't want her peeping in it. So she was told!

That was the perfect time for him to forget about it! Right after a group of guys told his soon to be spouse that he's the biggest liar on earth. The sight of it just sitting there on the night stand made her extra curious. She opened it and gazed at his driver's license. She removed it and calmly placed the wallet back onto the night stand. She became very upset but kept her cool while sitting on the bed. He came out of the bathroom about five minutes later.

"How old did you say you were?" she asked.

"What?" he asked in return.

"I said how old are you?"

"Stop playing!" He said while giggling slightly.

"Do I look like I'm playing?" She said with a very serious look on her face.

"No, and I told you how old I was! Didn't I?"

"Well, can you tell me why your license says that you're ten years older than what you told me?" she asked while holding it up.

He was speechless. I can imagine he was scared too; scared of having objects flung at his head. Amazingly though, she remained calm. Thirty seconds passed and he still hadn't given her an answer. She burst into tears.

"How could you lie to me about this? The whole time we've been together you've been lying about your age! What else have you lied about? Is all that stuff they've been saying about you true?"

"No!" he answered.

"How do I know that? Why did you lie about your age?"

There was another long pause, and then he spoke, "because I didn't think you would want me if you knew my real age."

That answer must have struck a sympathy nerve. In other words, she felt sorry for him. She got even softer when he squeezed a couple of tears out. He then gave a tale of bad things that happened earlier in his life. I wonder why! He spoke of awful treatment by his family and other people always putting him down. He lacked confidence and self esteem while growing up. He went on and on and on until her eyes were full of tears again. She got extremely soft on him. She found a way to compromise with his newly revealed age.

Remember the lesbian who wanted to do the background check? Well, she did it at her own expense. She uncovered some shocking information, but never told my wife exactly what it was. There was a comment made about checking his marital status. That caused my wife's curiosity to soar. There was a need to know the whole truth before the relationship could move any further. She became her own private investigator. And what better place to start investigating other than at his family's!

It didn't take long to get in touch with them. When it was revealed, she visited the town where he grew up. Everybody knew everybody and they especially knew him. Hardly any time had passed before everything started coming to light.

When she first met him, he said he only had two younger

children. That was another lie. He had seven and possibly more; mostly sons. Even had some as old as my ex. Did he have grandchildren? You betcha! A whole bunch of em! He once told her, "Man, you gotta lot of kids!" He failed to mention he had nearly two times as many as she had, that he knew of.

Another big surprise is he really didn't own all those things. Whoa, big surprise! He was just another regular ole Joe. He'd always go out of the way to impress others; even if it took extreme lying.

Next came the most serious lie of them all. The lie that set the stage for the next round of happenings! This kind of untruth might be the most dangerous that could be told in a relationship. It has caused individuals to get physically harmed and/or killed. A lot of lives have been ruined because of it. I think you all know which one I'm describing.

The background checking lesbian told my soon to be ex to check his marital status. That she did; very adamantly. She spoke with his mom and to whoever else would talk. She not only found that he was still married, but that he had two wives prior to the present one. Eligible bachelor huh! Never been married; right! He and his present wife were separated and in the process of divorcing. She was living with some other guy and may have been pregnant by him. It was understood that my wife's fiancé had major problems in each marriage. He almost lost his life during the first one. His first wife shot him! Can you see why he needed extra time before asking my wife to marry him?

To this day, I believe he really cared for my wife at one point in their relationship. His mistake was using deceit to attract and hold on to her. Honesty is the best policy; especially when dealing with my wife. I know this!

There is no need to describe how all this made her feel. I'm pretty sure we all know. The words angry, mad, irate, heated, furious, enraged, and infuriated are all extreme understatements. I won't bother using them. Her feelings were indescribable. Surprisingly though, she didn't bother showing how she felt about it at that time. Not even when confronting him about it.

Of course he was angry that the truth was manifested through his family. All-that Private I biz made him want nothing else to do with her. He expressed that to her over, and over again. Still she remained cool and collective the whole time. That would have scared me to death if I was him. How could anyone remain so calm after being so badly deceived? It was because she had something big planned for him. If you ask me, this is when a person is most dangerous in one way or another. They make you think all is ok, then "BAM"! You don't know what hit you.

She called the hotel where he was staying one day. She spoke with the front desk and got the name of one of his co-workers who was there also. She could be very persuasive if need be. That co-worker was a complete stranger and knew nothing of her. She never contacted him but needed his name for a reason. It was used to assist with something very evil and cunning.

She made a phone call to her fiancé's job and spoke with management. She pretended to be a front desk employee at the hotel. She boasted about that co-worker whose name she got, but never met.

"Oh he's very nice and respectable," she said.

But not her fiancé, his reputation got trashed.

"He disrespects us all the time," she said. "He's very nasty and never nice. He harasses all the women here. I think he's a pervert or sexual predator or something!"

Those were serious allegations. It really got their attention. To top it off, she called back an hour later with more.

"I am so shaken up!" she said frantically. "I was walking in the hallway, and he called me over to his door! He said he needed help with something! When I got there, he was completely naked! He was actually naked in the doorway and holding up his penis with a knife! He asked me if I wanted it! I screamed and he closed the door! I've never been so disgusted in my life!"

They tried to get her to file a sexual harassment claim. She told them no because she didn't want him to get fired. Too late for that huh! Her whole purpose was to get him fired. He caused her pain, so she tried to repay the favor. She figured he loved his job most of all because that's mainly what he talked about. Her actions almost backfired though.

"Some woman at the hotel is trying to get me fired!" he told her. "She told my boss I tried to rape her!"

"Really!" my wife said. "Do you know who it was?"

"No! They're talking about suspending me and doing an investigation! These guys are jealous of me too and hate me like everybody else at that job! Why would somebody lie on me like that? I did nothing to nobody at that hotel! Why are they messing with me?"

It took all her strength to keep from laughing. The pain in his voice delighted her so much, that she allowed this to go on for a couple of weeks. She didn't care if he lost his job or not. She wanted him to hurt as much as he hurt her. He called her constantly about it for the whole two weeks. He actually cried while on the phone with her. She almost had compassion for him and almost gave herself away. But the truth always comes out on its own.

"It was you!" he said after she answered the phone one evening.

"What are you talking about?" she asked.

"I know it was you! That call didn't come from the hotel! It didn't even come from that city! It came from your town! I know you did it!"

"You don't know nothing!" she yelled.

They had their worst argument yet. He kept accusing and she kept on denying. They both used those curse words I don't think I ever heard before. He completely put her down and belittled her. He spoke as if she was beneath the scum of the earth. Don't know exactly what was said, but something triggered her into admitting she was the guilty one. Guess she wanted him to see what she was capable of if crossed the wrong way. Still, it nearly backfired.

"Hello," I answered the phone.

"I need to ask you something!" she said anxiously.

"Calm down! What's the matter?"

"Can a person get arrested for calling someone's job and lying on them?"

"I don't know about getting arrested, but I think they can be sued for slander or something. What did you do?" I asked.

She explained everything that happened. He kept calling her and threatened to have her put in jail. I think he did it to make her as scared as he was when he thought he was losing his job. It was a revenge thing. He had her to write his job a letter stating that she made the whole thing up. He was supposed to stop bothering her about it afterward but didn't. She was truly afraid of being arrested and it bothered her day and night. Fortunately though, it never happened. He eventually stopped bothering her about it. One would think this incident ended everything; but think again. It wasn't over just yet.

For some unexplained, idiotic reason, she still wanted to be with this guy. He asked for the ring back and didn't want to see her anymore. However, she wasn't willing to let go so easily.

Her business was doing terrible with very small profits. She'd round up whatever cash that could be found and used it to visit him. The visits were unexpected but he treated her extra nice when she got there. I didn't blame him for being cautious of her. The things he did made her unpredictable. His fear of her was only human nature, so he totally respected her in person. He didn't come to see her anymore at all. There was an attempt to avoid her in any way possible. The goal was to cause her to lose whatever feelings she had left for him without a major confrontation. Her goal was to retrieve the feelings back he use to have for her. It was like a game of push and pull. He wanted to be rid of her but she would not let him go.

I've heard of others not wanting to let go although they knew it was the best thing to do. They felt that too much time was invested in the relationship to just let it go to waste. They tried to stick with it no matter how bad they got treated by the other person. It's weird, but it happens.

My soon to be ex found out how difficult it was reeling him back in. She felt it was time for a different strategy; something that would give him no choice but to fall back in love with her. She thought doing things for his family would work. They were given gifts and other materials they needed. She ran errands and went out of the way for them. But all she got from him was a "thank you". Not one feeling for her returned.

Her acts of kindness made him recognize that she wasn't going to let up anytime soon. He had to get hostile and it had to be done quickly.

He kept avoiding her in person but restarted answering the phone when she called. That is when the beast within him came out. This guy cursed out and disparaged her every chance he got. He called her every bad thing that a woman could be called. She was being torn down to the floor. She fought back but the battle cries were false. She still wanted to be with him. Her mind and character was being destroyed. For about a month, she was in tears every time I saw her. I knew what was happening but she refused to discuss it. Anyone who asked about it would get snapped at.

Yes, bitterness had set in and it was aimed at everyone but him. I stopped speaking to her for fear of being lashed out at. There were almost physical skirmishes with folks she'd never had problems with. It was all because of that guy. Talking to her was like talking to a rubber ball. Words bounced right off of her and back to you. The truth only made her angrier. Words were not going to make her see the light, so I prayed for her.

We've all gone through situations comparable to this. You know, completely focused on something we know we can't or shouldn't have. We may become relentless, and then something steps in and breaks it. It's the one thing we're not willing to put up with. It will cause us to let loose of whatever we think we can't live without.

This guy wasn't the biggest dummy in the world. He figured out what it would take to get this problem off his back. He stopped verbally abusing her on the phone. It took her a while to notice it. The phone conversations became pleasant again. They talked about everything just like in the beginning. They were back, so she thought; until an unexpected comment was made.

"Man, that woman didn't want me to leave last night," he said.

"Woman! What woman?" my wife asked.

"Oh, I didn't tell you about my new girlfriend."

"No! This is my first time hearing about her!"

At first, she thought he was just saying it to help push her away. If it were true, she would cut him loose without thinking twice about it. It's a part of her belief system. No dating him if he's with another woman. His wife was no concern because they were separated and going through a divorce. Plus, she was pregnant by and living with another man.

My soon to be ex had to be for certain that he was dating someone else. She went back into private eye mode. It took maybe a week to find that it was true. They had actually been dating longer than she thought. Almost immediately after she tried to destroy his career! The new woman was that thing that stepped in and broke her quest to get him back. They were done for. We all knew it because she started being nice to us again. It's funny how she didn't remember treating us so nasty like. They never do, right? They prance around thinking they can do no wrong and no one should ever have an issue with them. No matter what they've done! And she did a lot of dirt.

Her feelings for him subsided, but the two remained friends even until this day. They often consult each other on subjects regarding everyday life. Mainly about the opposite gender and relationships; including her new ones. Yes, she dated other men after him. Who would've thought it?

"Why so soon?" people asked. "She left her husband for another man, and now has broken it off with him! That wasn't so long ago, but she's already dating! Leaving her husband was so stupid!" Those were some of the same folks who said she should try that other man; her new ex-fiancé. It's amazing how things turn around!

There was more to it than just dating the other guys. I think she did it to prove to herself that she was truly over her ex fiancé. She was extra careful, not too quick in allowing her feelings to get caught up with them. It seemed to be all about having fun. Nothing serious or physical, just having fun.

It all played out within a few months. She suddenly lost interest in all those other men. We had already finalized our divorce, but she set her focus back on me for some reason.

"I wanna get back with you," she'd say some times when she visited.

I wasn't the least bit interested. There were no feelings left for her in my entire body. Don't get me wrong, I still cared for her as a friend. But there was no chance of that kind of relationship brewing back up. It just wasn't there anymore. Still she tried her best to get back in with me.

"Think about the children!" she'd say.

That was the same thing I told her before she stepped out on us. How ironic is that?

She acknowledged her big mistake and claimed to others that she wanted her family back. People were listening, especially those who kept poking their noses in. You know, the folks that said she should try that other guy, later called her stupid for leaving me! They poked again and said she shouldn't give up on me. What they failed to see was her lack of sincerity.

I knew exactly what her motives were. She needed redemption, which would have relaxed her conscience. It might have gotten rid of all the guilt that was burdening her. She was also hoping for something else. Allowing her to come back in would've made her look like an angel in everyone's eyesight. That was more important to her than anything at the time. I guess nobody could blame her. Who wouldn't wanna look good after making the most foolish decision of their life?

Like I said, there was a lack of sincerity. She didn't love me and I didn't love her either; not in that way. My true feelings were expressed loud and clear without a trace of confusion. Most of the time however, it took an argument in order for hers to be expressed. She would retract them afterward. But I knew how she really felt about me. I'd start a squabble purposely just to hear her say it. I should've recorded some of the awful insults aimed at me. Maybe she would have remembered them for a change.

She eventually gave up and let me go on with my life. She said everything I told her about that guy came true. I could have said, "Told ya so!" but didn't. He put her through almost as much drama as she put me through. Not without biting the bullet though! He too had to endure her fury once everything was brought to light. They both discovered they weren't that compatible after all.

It was now time to put it all to rest. We were delighted that it was all over with. Things had changed; it was time to make the proper adjustments in our lives. Bonds were broken and created. My ex-wife became my new friend, and they remained friends like stated above.

People marveled at my ex and me because of our friend-ship. How was it possible after all that has happened? Other couples have had similar experiences, but can't stand to look at each other. That's because they have no desire to exist in peace. We have peace because of GOD and because of our children. That's all that needs to be said about it!

CHAPTER 10

The Good Of It All

THE BIBLE SAYS that all things work together for our good, if we love GOD. I found this to be true even when things based on the Bible take a turn downhill. Things such as marriage! If you've been there, you know that breakups and divorces are very painful and depressing. We experience some of the most awful feelings that could ever be felt. Tears are shed and there is a belief that life is just about over for us. Well, that's the way I felt when I split with my wife! It was like the worst thing that could happen in life. The chances of there being a silver lining or a rainbow were zero to none. So I thought. But all things work together for our good like stated above.

Have you ever had one of those moments when your life flashes before your eyes? You remember events, good and bad, that took place in your past. Something similar happened to me. Let's just say my marriage flashed before my eyes. It happened soon after I was advised by GOD to, "JUST LET GO!" It was a little something to help me get through the whole thing. Come to think of it, that memory flash assisted me with the letting go process most of all.

I was lounging around thinking about how much I hated her when it took place. The bad episodes in my marriage were rivaled against the good. I think we all know which group won. It actually became a one sided battle. The bad whipped the good ragged. I revisited nearly all the negative events that I endured in my marriage. I was also taken back to a few pre-marital incidents which could've been used as warning signals. Warnings to not marry her of course!

All those past experiences caused me to do some serious thinking; but one stood out the most. It never came across my mind while we were together. Guess it took something severe enough to happen in order for it to enter into my thought waves.

So what was this thing that was illuminating my mind like a lighthouse? It was progress. People expect to advance when they get married, right? Not only in finances, but in the relationship too. Should they be willing to sacrifice and budget early on in order to provide for their family in the future? Should they be willing to give up bad habits and certain routines so that it would be more tolerable for them to live together? My answer to both these questions is yes!

Anyhow, I realized there wasn't a lot of progress in my marriage. I was completely willing to sacrifice and budget whatever finances we had. My ex-wife can witness to that because I was always on her about doing it too. But she always refused to, and felt it was impossible for some strange reason. Even after opening her store. There was very, very little financial progress between us.

As for relationship progress, I nearly did a complete three-sixty. I mean, I did a lot of changing both inside and out. I instantly stopped doing some things that got on her nerves when she expressed her dislike of them. I'm not trying to make her out as the only bad guy, because there are other things I could have changed that would've helped. But she never put much of an effort into making our union more delightful. Not a lot of progress in the relationship either!

Yeah, our breakup and divorce was terrible. That's one way to look at it. Now that I've had more time to think about it, I would argue that it was something good. Since the divorce, we both have been able to progress on our own. We've been able to get ahead in many different facets of life. Our children are getting more of what they need and are doing more than they've ever been able to do in the past. Now think about this! Is a marriage really meant to be when there is hardly any forward movement? Especially after ten years in it. I'll let everyone answer that for themselves.

I've often heard that bad things happen in order to prepare us for something bigger and better. I'm a firm believer of that. I realized it happened to me a few times during the early years of my marriage. Here's some examples; two former jobs.

I worked at this one job for about a year and wasn't too thrilled about it. The pay wasn't good and it was not the field I wanted to be working in. Yet I stayed with it. My performance was just as good as any of the other employees. I did my job one hundred percent like it was supposed to be done. Then I came in one day just to find that I was wrongfully ousted. There were no ill feelings toward that employer. Matter of fact, there was a sense of freedom and relief. I kept believing something positive would come of it. A couple of months later I was at another job. It was exactly what I was looking for. The pay was excellent and the work environment was second to none.

I know bigger and better things will come, if we remain patient and hold on to that belief. That second job was proof of that. Divorce was horrible, but it prepared us for a pleasant future.

Now, about being patient! Patience probably would have kept me from making one of my biggest mistakes. Let's just face the facts. I jumped into a relationship and got married too soon. I didn't know my mate as well as I thought and I failed to count up the costs of being married. Neither of us was prepared to make that step. We jumped right in just like millions of other couples did. We neglected to get ready for one of the greatest changes in life. The most important part of this readying process is to seek GOD first about it. That we didn't do!

I believe there would be far less divorces if people sought him prior to making the big hitch. GOD would let us know if we're making a mistake or not. Although he honors marriages, it doesn't mean that they all should have taken place. Without his approval prior to the event, they seem to have everlasting troubles. Those troubles vanish when the couple splits. My ex-wife and I can testify to that.

We've been getting along better than ever. Maybe this is a sign that we should have only been friends from the beginning. When I first met her, my intentions were not to go beyond a friendship anyway. Regrettably I did. Our problems started when we started dating and they remained with us the whole time. No couple can say their marriage is perfect, but you must admit; some of the dilemmas I had with my wife were out of the ordinary. I'm sure others have gone through some of the same type of stuff, but I've never heard of it. Not until I started dating her.

So am I sad that I am divorced now? No! Not at all! My ex isn't either! Just the thought of being single again is refreshing. Especially after coming from a bad marriage! I remember first feeling that way on the day of our court hearing.

We met with the lawyer outside of the courtroom after we were dismissed. Only one lawyer was needed since we were in complete agreement and not contesting anything. It sounded weird but it felt so good when the attorney shook our hands and said, "Congratulations! You two are single again!" I felt like jumping through the roof. My ex had the biggest smile on her face; couldn't remember when I last saw that. Our friendship was renewed and we haven't looked back since. See! Things that look bad can end up being good.

Over the years, I've watched person after person learn lessons from making big mistakes. They put their guards down, then get hurt or ripped off by others. The suffering brings on a curiosity. We tend to develop an interest in those things that we've had negative contacts with. We try to learn as much as we can about whatever it was and hope to never make that mistake again. Well, at least I do! I know others have also. Here are two examples.

One, we see it on television all the time. You know, when animals attack. Some are domestic, some are wild beast attacks. What do the survivors of these attacks tell us when we see them on the screen again? They say they have a greater respect for that species. They also learned a great deal about the animal hoping to avoid any future attacks.

Two, you invest in some business because it sounds legitimate. Some months later, you discover that the con-artist who proposed it to you is nowhere to be found. You were straight-up scammed. What do you do? You learn all you can about the type of business, you thought you were investing in, regardless if you continue to pursue it or not. Also, you teach yourself to spot a schemer afar off. When these types of things come at you again, you'll know exactly which direction to run.

Now let's get back to me. My suffering brought on an interest in relationships. I learned as much as I could about them; mainly from listening to others. Different aspects of it can be discussed. However; I feel that the do's and don'ts are the most important. I'll give some examples of the ones I've learned and experienced.

One hundred percent honesty at the beginning is the best policy. That's one hundred percent honesty, no exceptions. An individual may feel there's something in his/her past that's just too awful to reveal. He/she believes that if it were told to the one being pursued, it would ruin the chances of ever being with that person. So he/she lies about it and hopes to carry it to the grave. But what if the truth does get revealed? Then what? You could be happily married to someone going on twenty-five good years; just living a wonderful life. All of a sudden, the truth comes out unexpectedly. The happy days are over and your marriage is just about finished. This is all because you couldn't tell the truth about one little thing in the beginning.

Think about this! Wouldn't it have been better to be honest at the start and take a chance of never even getting with that person; or building up so much over the years only to watch it all disappear in the twinkle of an eye? Which would be better? I think I know everyone's answer! Nobody wants their life to be a soap opera. Well, most of us don't. There might be a few odd balls in the world. Anyhow, complete honestly is a must do.

I stated earlier how I found this out the hard way after telling small lies; at the beginning!

Now let's discuss a "don't". Both the husband and wife have responsibilities and duties in a marriage. Some are interchangeable if you ask me. What's wrong with the man cooking sometimes or the woman taking out the trash every once in a while? Sometimes it's necessary to switch. Responsibilities will be no problem as long as they remember marriage is a fifty-fifty thing. Obviously, some spouses forget about equality in a marriage; or don't believe there is any. One may feel that he/she should be in complete control of certain things. Things, such as the way money is spent in the home.

Of course that was one of the biggest problems I had with my ex. At first I couldn't understand why she felt she should handle the finances. She was always terrible with money. Later I discovered she was just simply money crazy. She'd often say we would never be able to save any money. Which wasn't the case at all; she just didn't want to. Any cash left over, after all the needs were met, she would mess it all off. A bunch of unnecessary wasting and spending! We'd be broke by the next payday.

Many times, her hunger to spend wildly caused us to get behind on rent and other bills. I gave her the money to pay them on time, but she didn't. A purse or a pair of shoes was more important. Once, I tried to introduce her to a budget plan I knew would work. She wanted no part of it. The plan would have interfered with her non-stop shopping habits. She said she wasn't listening to me and the plan went in one ear and right out the other. Yeah, she was in complete control!

Taking care of the children and other household work should be shared equally as well. It's all about love and respect. If both spouses spend a decent amount of time with the children, most likely their offspring will love and respect them the same. Shared work around the home also brings on love and respect. The trouble starts when one wants to be in control. This control is when one spouse slacks and allows the other to do most of the household chores. The slacking spouse feels that it is more important to hang out with friends or to relax than see to the needs of the home. The good spouse is left with the bulk of the work even after being at a job for eight hours. He/she might allow the slacking to go on for a while, but it gets old real quick. Then it's time to fight about it!

So don't ever allow the other person to be in complete control of anything! It could be seen as a sign of weakness. I allowed it to happen in my home; therefore I take partial blame for some of the unwise things my ex did. My unwillingness to stand up and be a man was taken advantage of.

COMMUNICATION, COMMUNICATION, and more COMMUNICATION! Need I say more? No, but I will! A lack of good communication is one of those straws that break the camel's back. If it leaves and never returns, it will most likely spark the end of the relationship. It is a must have in any type of relationship. Even one with GOD requires good communication. There's certain things he won't do for you unless you ask; and how will you know what he wants you to do without talking to him? It has been proven that marriages last longer when spouses communicate more than often. They are able to talk anytime about anything.

I'm not a communication expert but I know it's very important. My belief is that it has something to do with attention. All of us want attention from our significant other. If a person doesn't, then there's something wrong with him/her. Communication was brought up during the counseling session my ex and I had with our pastor. He said he talked with his wife whenever she wanted to. He would shut off the TV, even if watching his favorite show, to talk to her. It was all about giving her attention.

I take half the blame for the communication breakdown in my marriage. It was excellent at one point, but stuff happens. I question if it would have helped us had it remained solid. Good communication is definitely a vital must do.

Couples having daily conversations about daily occurrences are a good mode of communication. Yes it is, but not the only good mode. When a person has a house built, they expect the builder to use high quality construction materials. This will help it stand the test of time and endure the changing weather conditions. Also a person with a healthy lifestyle will consume food that's healthy for the body. It keeps them looking good and reduces the risk of disease. These high quality materials and healthy foods are like words couples use to build each other up. This communication will increase the lifeline of the marriage. Using bad and abusive words toward each other is like building a house with poor materials and eating nothing but bad food. Sooner or later it will all fall apart. Everyone wants to be built up, not broken down. Two tools to build with are complimenting and supporting.

I think complimenting is the more important of the two. That's just my opinion though. Flattering your spouse assures her/him that she/he still has your attention. It has to at least be done on a daily basis. Feel free to do it multiple times a day; it won't hurt anything. Trust me! It was one of the biggest issues during our break-up. My ex said the lack of it was a powerful force that helped push her into the arms of the other man. I don't disagree that it contributed to her leaving me, but I actually never stopped complimenting her. She either didn't hear or receive them when I did it. She still can't remember. Anyhow, not showering your mate with flattering remarks might cause her/him to seek them from others. We all desire to be admired and built up at all times.

So how often should we support each other? In all that we do of course. As long as it doesn't harm anybody in any form or fashion. What does support from spouses mean? It means they have their mates' best interest at heart. Support encourages and increases confidence. It can also create confidence that wasn't there at first. Take my ex for instance. At first, she did not believe she could open a store and run it successfully. No faith at all! I said I would support her in all ways possible. I would give my time and last penny to help if I had to. She became a new person at that very moment. Nothing in the world was going to stop her from accomplishing this goal. And it didn't!

See; non-stop support is another must do. And you can't just say it; you have to show action too. Let's say your mate was trying to lose twenty pounds. He/she goes out and walks ten miles every other day. You say you're going to support, and you go out and walk with him/her also. What does that do for your mate? It shows that you really care and it keeps your mate striving to reach that goal. You two also develop a stronger bond.

No bond is immune to collapsing however. Each one has the possibility of being broken by something. There are marriages which have endured every arrow that was shot their way. Others came close but got taken out by arrows carrying extra ammo. This ammunition could be something that influences a spouse one way or another. Or it could simply be someone trying to interfere with the relationship. This brings us to another don't.

Don't, except for three exemptions, allow anyone into your personal business at home. These three exemptions are marital counselors, family, and good friends. Just be sure to be extra careful when inviting in the latter two. It is imperative to know if they are really there to help and not harm you any further. If to harm is the motive, then don't let them in under any circumstances.

Both I and my ex were guilty of that. I allowed family in, she let family and friends come in. They, in some fashion, assisted with the demise of our marriage. Mainly with rumors and gossiping that developed from info we gave them. They didn't even have to be there in the flesh to have an impact on our life. Some were hundreds of miles away and still able to cause contentions between me and my ex. Just by spreading lies and rumors that got back to us. Some of these folks actually hurt themselves just to see us fail. They destroyed their own relationships when they poked their noses into ours. But they didn't care just as long as they could see the wedge driven between us. Some people are just plain pitiful! So you better think about it before trusting friends and family with your personal business.

The last and most important must do I can think of, is keeping

GOD in your marriage. The family that prays together stays together! That is absolutely true. You remember all those problems in my marriage that I stated earlier? By allowing GOD in and praying together, we managed to keep our marriage afloat. It sunk when we neglected to pray. A lack of prayer will damage that protective shield GOD has around you. A small crack is all the devil needs to sneak in and do his dirty work. The Bible says GOD honors marriages. Because of that, Satan will do all he can to destroy them. Just look at the high divorce rate in the world. Of course it's greater among unions which don't involve GOD at all. These include people who get hitched just to be doing something. They never consider the true purpose of matrimony and treat it like leasing a vehicle. When they are done with it, they let it go and look for another. Hollywood is well known for that.

Keeping GOD in your marriage will not only keep it together, but will also help in other areas. He will lead and guide us to make wiser decisions. We all know that one of the main causes of divorce is finances. Some couples live above their means to try to impress or keep up with others. They get into financial chaos and have a hard time dealing with the pressure. You know what happens next. The arguments begin and divorce will more than likely follow; if the LORD is not in their lives. I'm sure all couples have made some kind of monetary mistake. But I know GOD will bring you out before it gets too bad and everything starts to break down. He's able to get you to a point where you won't make those blunders again.

GOD will even help you choose the right friends to socialize with. These will be true and won't do anything to harm your marriage. The ones we choose on our own may very well be our worst enemies. They're in that group which could have a nasty impact on your relationship with your spouse. I mentioned them earlier.

The LORD is the ultimate peacemaker. If you try him, you'll see that he's second to none when it comes to resolving conflicts. There will eventually be some conflict in the household.

But if he is there, they will all end peacefully. That may be the most important reason to allow GOD in your marriage.

Those were some things we could have done and should not have done to help our marriage. I'm sure there are others that could have been mentioned. Nevertheless, the idea is that these learned lessons were good points of my marriage. Anyone who reads this that's married or thinking about getting married should take them to heart. I'm no expert, but what harm could they possibly do? They can only help!

Yes! I was in a marriage for ten years that was mostly pickles and lemons instead of peaches and cream. It seemed all bad, but some good came out of it. I have four beautiful children which is the greatest that came from it. Another good thing is the experience. Trust me, ten years is a lot of it! I'm well prepared if I decide to do it all over again. For now, I'm just taking my time and enjoying the single life.

As for my ex wife, I'm not real sure. Maybe she learned her lessons, maybe she didn't. Only she can answer that. But I know she'll always remember the whole ordeal leading up to the end. Nobody could forget that. Especially the ones who stepped out instead of staying home and attempting to work through the problems! They think trouble at home is their justification for trying new and better things. My ex tried it and found herself floating on cloud nine at first. It was so exciting as she was having the time of her life. She failed to realize no bad deed goes unpunished. So did her boyfriend. Although feelings might have developed for her, it was still wrong. When all the chips fell, they both discovered they were in forbidden waters. A territory they vowed to enter no more.

We are the only beings on GOD's earth who are given a choice to either do right or wrong. Some decisions we make on our own, others are altered by outside forces. Regardless, it's still up to the individual on which path to choose. So when we take actions that we regret in the future, we can blame nobody but ourselves. We should take more time to think about it and count up the costs while we're looking over the fence. We should ask ourselves, "Is the grass really greener?" Don't end up like my ex wife! She had an opportunity to do the right thing but didn't. She did **think** about it and it looked all good. She wanted to take a chance which caused her to **leap** over the fence. The grass looked greener for a while. Then it dried up and turned brown. She ended up in the state called **regret**!

THE END

www.ingramcontent.com/pod-product-compliance
Lightning Source LLC
Chambersburg PA
CBHW030344290526
45785CB00004B/1587